A Leader's Call

King David

MICHAEL P. WATERMAN

ISBN 978-1-64191-127-6 (paperback)
ISBN 978-1-64299-642-5 (hardcover)
ISBN 978-1-64191-128-3 (digital)

Christian Faith Publishing, Inc.
832 Park Avenue
Meadville, PA 16335
www.christianfaithpublishing.com

Printed in the United States of America

This book is dedicated to my mother, Janet Waterman (12/26/1936–01/22/2010). Her courage battling with cancer is what inspired the book you are about to read. The example she exhibited during death helped allow the Holy Spirit to lead me closer to the Most High. Mom, this book is for you.

Thank you for all of your sacrifice and selflessness. It will always be treasured.

I miss you more and more as the years advance. It is my hope and prayer to become a man of faith and passion like King David. My hope's desire is to be a man after the heart of God.

I want all to think of you as the woman in this picture. You will always be loved and remembered.

Contents

Contents

Glossary

Throughout this book, the names of God will be capitalized.
Lord, Hashem, Most High, Jehovah, Almighty, Father, High Tower, Omnipotent One, Messiah, Creator, Yahweh, Mighty One.

Prologue

It is an honor and privilege to write the prologue for a book. This is especially true when considering the topic: King David, what a subject!

In this book, King David's life is uniquely examined. The ups, the downs, and everything in-between are discussed. It is a call to all in any area of leadership. You see; all of us are leaders in a certain area of life.

"A Leaders Call", will inspire your heart about why leadership is essential to all. This is a topic for individuals, families, and organizations on how to radically set your life on a positive course.

Reading this book showed me the heart of David, the heart of God, and my own heart. Please allow the questions at the end of each chapter to challenge the depths of your heart.

I have known Michael for over 20 years. We have had a friendship that has only grown stronger throughout the years. We have both been through many rodeos that life had thrown at us. I see so much of what we experienced in this book. It is so relatable and timely.

Character in the modern leader is sorely lacking. Looking at a man, known as having a heart after the Lord's, shows how leaders should be.

Michael and I have shared many great experiences working hard serving many people from diverse backgrounds. One great lesson we have learned is that we could not have endured these challenges without having a strong belief in the Most High, devotion to his word and a strong spiritual relationship. I can honestly say that we are more than friends; we are brothers.

We both had the opportunity to be caregivers to dying parents. This experience taught both of us that all that we are able to truly hold onto is the same God that King David worshipped.

I encourage you to allow this book, inspired by God, to transform your heart and make you a leader like that of King David.

George A. Shaw
Roanoke, VA
The Voice of the Audio Book

Introduction

King David: A Man after God's Own Heart!

What a life to examine. What a life to learn from. What a life to emulate. King David, the greatest king in the history of this world. His life was worthy of study and examination.

It should be our aim in this life to be known as one who is, "A man or woman after God's own heart."

What a challenge.

This man's life shows us the heart that the Lord seeks. He was a leader that deeply desired to please the Almighty God. His passion and heart's truest desire was to bring glory to Hashem.

He was known as a man after the heart of God. The Most High himself handpicked David to lead his most treasured possession — his chosen people — the Israelites.

He was a leader who needs to be replicated in today's morally decayed society. He was a man who had high integrity and ethical morals. He was a leader who truly led by example. His heart was soft, and desiring to please the Most High. He genuinely knew that the buck stopped with him. He was not in the custom of making excuses. He was quick to repent and had a humble, teachable heart.

This book is a call and a warning for all leaders. It is a warning and a challenge in all areas of life. In sincere honesty it is a call to all. It is a call to have the heart of a true leader.

In this introduction, it is my intention to clarify that this book, and faithfully this entire five-part book series, has one main directive:

to call you, the reader, to deal with your heart. The title is "A Leader's Call". In a sense, we are all leaders. This book, inspired by the Most High, is being written to wake us up. The state of leaders in our society has become a sad and shallow representation of what the sacred scriptures declare.

The Leader's Call is to be a man or woman after the heart of God. It does not matter in which area your profession lies. It is of no consequence your standing according to the world's standards. It is not a matter of your tax bracket or job title. Your age, race, ethnicity, gender, and educational background are trivial. Your political view is of no matter. We are called to be men and women of more noble character.

We are to be like the Bereans:

> *These people were more willing to listen than the people in Thessalonica. The Bereans were eager to hear what Paul and Silas said and studied the Scriptures every day to find out if these things were true. (Acts 17:11, NCV)*

We are to be eager to learn, study, and examine daily, the only beneficial literature to see if what is preached out there is true. The scriptures are to be our only belief system. They are to be our standard for life. All else in this life is of little use.

My first boss after college used to tell me, and recently reinforced, that an idea is a dime a dozen. Those who truly listen and follow through with it are worth millions. Please be one of the few who take this biblical truth and run with it.

Let me ask you a question. When tragedy or suffering knocks at your door, who is the One you seek help from?

Are you in the habit of praying to your income, political view, tax bracket, or anything else so many idolize?

Do you pray to celebrities?

I didn't think so.

When we think of leadership in any area, what most often comes to mind?

Unfortunately, they are not positive. We think of corruption, greed, and hypocrisy. The term "two-faced" is often the reality of the leaders in this present age. In all areas of life, leaders with integrity and high moral fiber are hard to find.

Consider the political realm dominated by low character people pleasers who lost their sense of morals and ethics long ago. They sell out, and sell themselves to the highest bidder. This is why it is so difficult for there to be any true progress or growth. This explains the decreasing level of integrity suffered in each successive generation.

What comes to mind in the corporate world?

Most often, that world is associated with greed and scandal. They are led by greed to a deep lust for more and more profit at any and every cost. They are often accused of being heartless. They are those who often believe they are above the law.

No one is above God's Law!

How about in the religious world?

This will be the main focus of this book. By Faith, this will be the start of a five-book series pointing us to the God of David.

When asked about what comes to mind when thinking about religious leaders, people most often respond that they're hypocrites. They are called swindlers who take advantage of others. They use the Lord as their business investment and retirement plan. I believe that in 2018, most religious leaders are similar to King Saul. We need today, more than any period, Godly leaders in all areas like King David.

I know someone whom I talk with often that was burnt by religion early in his life. He is still relatively young, and when he hears the term "pastor," he thinks of one term: "crook." He is of the opinion, that the pastor of today is one who takes advantage of others for their own selfish gain.

This book was inspired by my observation about the decreasing number of noble-hearted leaders in present times. I personally know a plethora of bad examples. It is in all areas of life. These examples are in the business sector, medical profession, legal realm, education system, and most assuredly, the culture of religion. It is a burning desire the Most High has put on my heart to declare the heart that he desires.

I speak with people every day. Most call themselves believers. In my life these past twenty plus years, it has been a daunting task to find those who truly know, and wholeheartedly follow the One True God. Those who truly and deeply practice what they preach. The sad part is that, like other areas of life, most tend to follow leaders who are corrupt and lack morals. The religious world is filled with those looking for a shortcut with the Lord. They believe false teaching and do not find the one they claim to be seeking. The results are the same as the world. The desire is for selfish gain and personal glory.

This book provides sermons and Bible studies for you, the reader. It has been a long time coming. It is also written to challenge your heart and mind in order for you to truly deal with the state of your heart. In order to gain anything in this spiritual life, it is imperative that we deal with our heart. This will be a consistent theme throughout this book and future undertakings. This is not a book for the faint of heart. It is not for the shallow or superficial. There is a great need for deep and transparent people.

We live in a world where it is challenging to find sincerity and integrity in any area of leadership.

David's son Solomon wrote:

> *Many people claim to be loyal, but it is hard to find a trustworthy person. (Proverbs 20:6, NCV)*

What a challenge and endeavor it is to do this; deal with our heart. This book is not for you to simply read and think about, but to deal with the very fabric of your soul. I guarantee that if you do this, your life will never be the same. I know far too many religious people who are spiritually bankrupt. Their lives are consumed with keeping up with the Joneses. They have lost the true meaning of faith and a real relationship with our Creator. Their hearts, over time, unfortunately become numb and hard to the call of the Most High. Their first love has been lost if it was ever truly found. I know of many whom after decades are consumed with the things of God, but not the Lord himself. If this is you, then praise God. This book is inspired by the Holy Spirit with your soul already prayed for. This book will either wake up slumbering souls or ignite souls to seek and find the true God from the scriptures.

I beg you please don't ignore the call of this book for radical change. If you read it without any effect, then your heart is in a much worse state than you thought.

It is impossible to be an effective leader if you're not a teachable student. The greatest leader and teacher is the Most High himself. We must first follow in order to lead. The challenge and goal is to follow Hashem's lead.

It will be like what James described:

> *Don't fool yourself into thinking that you are a listener when you are anything but, letting the Word go in one ear and out the other. Act on what you hear! Those who hear and don't act are like those who glance in the mirror, walk away, and two minutes later have no idea who they are, what they look like. (James 1:22–24, MSG)*

I would like to begin this endeavor with a question.
Who is your favorite figure from the Bible?

After spending twenty plus years daily reading the scriptures, my favorite figure from the sacred word is King David.
Why?

There are so many reasons.
In this book, I will frequently answer this question.

15

In this introduction, I will simply say that no matter where he was, how he was doing, how incredible the peaks, or how dreadful the lows, David would always turn back to his Heavenly Father.

He dealt with his heart!

In a time where true leaders are decreasingly rare, this is a man who lived a life worthy of our attention and emulation.

He was devoted to being one in Spirit with his God.

The challenge is for us to do the same.

What an example he was for us to follow.

This was the heart of David.

> *God, you are my God.*
> *I search for you.*
> *I thirst for you*
> *like someone in a dry, empty land*
> *where there is no water.*
> *I have seen you in the Temple*
> *and have seen your strength and glory.*
> *Because your love is better than life,*
> *I will praise you.*
> *I will praise you as long as I live.*
> *I will lift up my hands in prayer to your name.*
> *(Psalm 63:1–4, NCV)*

Before we open up and look at the life of this godly man, my question to you the reader; are you ready and willing to honestly deal with your heart, repent, and live a life worthy of what we are called to in the scriptures?

If yes, are you willing to make the Lord's sacred word your standard for living?

Why study King David?

David was such a relatable man. Just imagine your life being written for all eternity to see. All is laid bare. Nothing is hidden or sugar coated. Now consider the life of King David.

He was so real, raw and my so human. We are all able to relate with his life.

Consider the following about his life;

The way he prayed, wrestled with the Lord. He was an intense, fearless warrior in battle. He was a man of great passion. Even after sinning grievously, he knew that the God of Abraham, Isaac, and Israel was the one in charge. He knew intimately the God of all creation.

What comes to mind when thinking about King David?

There is so much to mention. Just consider:

There is the battle between David and Goliath. There is the incredible spiritual friendship between David and Jonathan. There is the conflict and major contrasts between David and Saul. There is the downfall from his adulterous affair with Bathsheba. There are the Psalms, the Ark of the Covenant, and the building of the Temple.

There is so much to learn from his incredible life. The challenge is to use his life written in the pages of scripture: the good, bad, and ugly (warts and all). The goal is to examine the scriptures and deal with your heart. This book is inspired for you, and not someone you know. Please don't just read it and move on.

In this book, it is my desire to look deeply and impartially at his life, his heart, and his relationship with our omnipotent, omniscient, sovereign, and perfect God.

Over the past two decades, I have read many books based on scripture. To say these books have enriched my life and my eternal destination is a tremendous understatement.

The goal in writing this book, as well as all of the influence that God has for me, is to point others to the scriptures. The hope is for others daily devotion to the holy word. The desire is for all to develop a true personal relationship with the Father through his Son the Messiah.

It is my goal to provide every scripture in its clearest translation. I want this to be a proverbial one stop shop with no distractions. This is a book through sermons and Bible studies I have personally used in the past. I have italicized the sermons. As you read the sermons, please imagine it being preached both to and for you. It is inspired by the word of God, and not my opinions.

The truth of scripture is described here:

> ***Most of all, you must understand this: No prophecy in the Scriptures ever comes from the prophet's own interpretation. No prophecy ever came from what a person wanted to say, but people led by the Holy Spirit spoke words from God. (2 Peter 1:20–21, NCV)***

At the end of every chapter, there are questions for you, the reader, to ponder and wrestle with. Please be painfully honest with yourself when answering before moving onto the next chapter. There will be a separate blank page for you to take notes. I implore you to answer all of the questions. Please, if possible, read and go over with others.

Please feel free to use this book for sermons, Bible studies, or to read and go through with others. It is my deepest prayer that the Holy Spirit uses it to convict, inspire, and lead you to make difficult decisions that bring about radical repentance and spiritual growth. Throughout this book it is my heart's desire to be open and transparent from my own life. I am so excited to see how the Lord uses this book in your life.

You are always in my prayers.

Remember who King David was known to be the father of.

> ***As Jesus went on from there, two blind men followed him, calling out, "Have mercy on us, Son of David!" (Matthew 9:27, NIV)***

Jesus was called the son of David. He could have been called son of Abraham, Isaac, or Israel.

Why David?

That is what we will study throughout this book.

This is my heart's prayer for you the reader as we begin this adventure together:

> *I have not stopped giving thanks to God for you. I always remember you in my prayers, asking the God of our Lord Jesus Christ, the glorious Father, to give you a spirit of wisdom and revelation so that you will know him better. I pray also that you will have greater understanding in your heart so you will know the hope to which he has called us and that you will know how rich and glorious are the blessings God has promised his holy people. (Ephesians 1:16–18, NCV)*

Let's start, 'A Leader's Call, King David.

Chapter 1

David the Beginning

We are about to embark upon a voyage that by faith will transform your life. It will lead you to a true knowledge and relationship, or a deeper one, with the Most High. It is not a journey to be taken lightly. This book serves several purposes. First, to examine a man of God whose life can deeply influence our own.

Second, it is going to point out differences in hearts. What I mean is throughout this book, we will see two types of hearts. The first heart we will see is the heart of the present-day leader. This heart is one of deceit, living a double life, and having no conscience or reverence toward God. This is a heart that never is dealt with. It is a heart unwilling or desiring to change. It is a heart full of pride and selfish ambition. It is a heart seeking the praise and glory that only belongs to the Lord.

The second heart is one like that of King David. This heart is one that deeply desires to be in step with Hashem. There is an openness and transparency that is accountable to the Lord. It is a heart that seeks humility and obedience. There is great failure, but with an earnestness to be right with the only true God. This heart is one of longing to be with God above all else.

A heart like this:

> *As a deer gets thirsty*
> *for streams of water,*
> *I truly am thirsty*

for you, my God.
In my heart, I am thirsty
for you, the living God.
When will I see your face? (Psalm 42:1–2, CEV)

The third is for you to decide which heart you now possess. The choice is then up to you.

Will you repent and follow the Most High as the scriptures declare, or will you continue living in opposition to him?

There will be no other choice.

King David lived a life of such great significance. We will look into most areas of his adventurous sojourn. We will study the highs, the lows, and the in-between.

In this, our first chapter together, we will begin our study before this man of God entered the scene.

We will commence our study with one another by going back into the past. We are going back over three thousand years. We will be looking at a point in time where it seems like a different planet. It is so long ago, yet in the spiritual realm, it is eerily similar to our day.

The fight against bad leadership and corruption is as old as time itself. There have always been politicians and leaders bent on greed. Our challenge is to have two visions at once. We are to see the simplicity of the rural and the life of old, as well as the heart of the modern-day leader.

In a sense, we are to live our lives with two directives. First, we are to seek after the truth. We are to seek to see through the eyes of the Most High.

Secondly, we must seek to uncover the counterfeit. They are at battle with one another. It has always been a battle between good versus evil.

This first chapter is from a sermon I have preached and taught to various groups. This first chapter's aim is to look at two men. These men are very different and have contrasting hearts. One is a man of God. A righteous spiritual leader we should aim to be like. The other is a clear and painful example of the type of modern leader we are to avoid becoming and following. As you read, take notice of the above. Be alert to see the battle of good versus evil, and deeply consider which side you reside.

In this first chapter, we begin in a tumultuous time in the history of God's people, Israel. Like today there was a lot of confusion.

Samuel, The Lord's Prophet!

When looking through a person's life especially a scriptural example in the likeness of King David, it is imperative to examine many criteria:

Where, when, what, and who influenced his destiny.

David was a shepherd of the sheep who played the harp. He was a man who loved the Lord with his all:

The command given to Moses:

> *Attention, Israel!*
> *GOD, our God! GOD the one and only!*
> *Love GOD, your God, with your whole*
> *heart: love him with all that's in you, love him*
> *with all you've got! (Deuteronomy 6:4–5, MSG)*

He was a poet, known as the psalmist. He was a warrior, a man tested in battle. He was a man filled with the Holy Spirit (more later about this one). He was the greatest king in the history of the world. He was a man of great passion, in everything he did.

As you read through the chapters, it will strike you that his experiences will seem quite familiar to the ones we deal with on a regular basis. Please look at the heart of the scriptures. They were written for all time. They were written for you.

Before studying the life of David, we must examine the state of God's chosen people: the Jews. The time before, there was a human king over the Israelites. In this chapter, we will be looking at the hearts of two men: The prophet Samuel and the first king, Saul. Please examine these men and ponder whom you are most like. At the end of this chapter, you will have your heart tested.

Who was Samuel?

Samuel was a faithful man, set apart by his mother Hannah. She was barren and pleaded with Hashem to be able to have a child.

So Hannah became pregnant, and in time she gave birth to a son. She named him Samuel, saying, "His name is Samuel because I asked the Lord for him." (1 Samuel 1:20, NCV)

The Lord honored this faithful mother's desperate prayer and plea to be delivered of her barrenness.

Samuel was the prophet of the Lord. He served the Lord for his entire life. He was a man of noble character. It was his heart's desire to see Jehovah praised and glorified. He saw the highs and lows of the people of God. He was the voice of Hashem, his prophet. He was a leader that we need to imitate. Samuel was the name of this judge, prophet, and godly man.

During his life, he had seen and experienced corrupt leadership. He had been the voice of the Lord. He had dealt with the fickleness of the Israelites' hearts. He had grown old. Unfortunately, his sons were corrupt and did not share the devotion he had to Hashem.

We begin our study at the point where the people of God wanted a king. They were never content following the true king. Not a man, but the Lord of Lord's and the God of all. His word and majesty were not what the people wanted. They were not content following the Most High.

It is amazing how real these scriptures are today. Take a moment and consider the religious culture of our time. It has become a personal choice of choosing what to believe and building a "god" to fit into our preferences. I often ask others which "god" is theirs. In reality it is a decision to make God the Lord and master of our lives.

It is here we find the aged prophet, Samuel. Please notice the heart he had for and toward Jehovah. We should all desire to have a heart like this prophet of the Lord.

1 Samuel 8:6–9 (New International Version)

The elders of Israel wanted a king.
They wanted to be the same as all of the other nations.
They were not satisfied having Jehovah, the Lord
God as their king.
God was not enough.
Samuel was the last judge, and was getting old.

But when they said, "Give us a king to lead
us," this displeased Samuel; so he prayed to the
Lord. (1 Samuel 8:6, NIV)

A good example when displeased, discouraged, hurt and angry; go pray!

In our present society, it is amazing how similar the religious world compares to Israel during Samuel's time. The religious world desires God on its own terms.

Please consider:

The Lord is not enough. The people want their own way.

We are so easily given to follow and believe false teaching and shallow worship.

It seems that in today's "Christian church," there are mainly two types of ministries. The first is either cheap grace, prosperity ministries focused on building and relying on self. The motivation is often greed and self-indulgence.

The other is a legalistic rules-oriented group. The life of the member is consumed with earning grace. The motivation is often power and control through manipulation and brainwashing.

There is either cheap grace or no grace. Neither bring honor to Hashem.

Unfortunately, for the most part, the focus is on man and false teaching with no commitment to the scriptures.

Take a minute and examine the news. Sporting events are can't miss. Concerts are displays of worship.

Consider the elaborate tributes and excessive praise given in the past few years to dead celebrities.

The worship of famous people!

Those whose lives are at war against the Most High are often worshipped.

More indicting, they worship those who often end up taking their own lives.

What a waste!

What a powerless empty waste!

Look at political rallies, man is God.

Consider all the racial turmoil. Think about all of the rampant violence and growing hate. Try to contemplate the proliferating instances of domestic violence.

How about the growing number of school shootings?

Our society is a mess.

It was the Lord's inspiration for the back cover.

Why in a leadership book about a godly man like King David are there pictures of Hitler, Stalin and the like?

Are their actions and atrocities condoned?

Absolutely not!

The reason is twofold. First, wickedness is not a trait we are born with. No one comes out of the womb bent on genocide. In the same way, no one is born a racist. No one just goes and shoots at schools and kills innocent children for no reason. If we are not alert and aware, we are just as able to create the next devil of this ilk. We need to wake up.

Second, the whole point of this life we live is to choose good or evil. We are to choose the type of leader we desire to be and, just as important, follow. The choice is either to become or follow a wicked leader, or to become or follow a leader like David and Samuel.

If we look at the decay of our society it stems from two deficiencies. We live in a world without God. False idols are everywhere. The second results from the first. There is a lack of godly men able or willing to confront corruption and evil.

To further examine this, let's ponder:

How about social media?

Millions follow those who are terrible examples.
How many proliferating followers do promiscuous women have?

How about athletes and entertainers who live adulterous and immoral lives?

Why?

How about the true state of the religious world?

The multitudes seek and follow mega church leaders. They chase after and allow these rejected false teachers to tell them what they want to hear rather than the truth.
They are being led astray!
So often the question to ask is what is your 'god' like?

The answer is disheartening.
Like Samuel, it is deeply painful for me to hear the response of Hashem through his spirit.
How about you?
Are you moved?
If not, what moves your heart?

> *7 And the Lord told him: "Listen to all that the people are saying to you; it is not you they have rejected, but they have rejected me as their king.*

We need to realize that when we get rejected from anyone while trying to please God, the one being rejected is God!
Remember who was doing the rejecting, the people of God, Israel.

Samuel described a later description of rejection for the coming Messiah prophesied by Isaiah:

> *He was despised and rejected—*

> *a man of sorrows, acquainted with deep-
> est grief.*
> *We turned our backs on him and looked
> the other way.*
> *He was despised, and we did not care.*
> *(Isaiah 53:3, NLT)*

Later the Apostle Peter was inspired to declare:

> *For it brings favor[y] if, mindful of God's
> will,[z][aa] someone endures grief from suffering
> unjustly. For what credit is there if you sin and
> are punished, and you endure it? But when you
> do what is good and suffer, if you endure it,
> this brings favor with God. (1 Peter 2:19–24,
> HCSB)*

Who are we to emulate?

> *For you were called to this,*
> *because Christ also suffered for you,*
> *leaving you an example,*
> *so that you should follow in His steps.*
> *He did not commit sin,*
> *and no deceit was found in His mouth;*
> *when He was reviled,*
> *He did not revile in return;*
> *when He was suffering,*
> *He did not threaten*
> *but entrusted Himself to the One who judges
> justly.*
> *He Himself bore our sins*
> *in His body on the tree,*
> *so that, having died to sins,*
> *we might live for righteousness;*

*you have been healed by His wounds. (1 Peter
2:21-24, HCSB)*

What do the people you deal with on a regular basis (family,
friends, co-workers, and religious organizations) seek from the Lord?

If you are honest, it is not often to feel rejection for trying to
serve the Omnipotent one.

*As they have done from the day I brought them
up out of Egypt until this day, forsaking me
and serving other gods, so they are doing to you.
(1 Samuel 8, NIV)*

We are the same.
*How often do we forsake the things of God to go after the things of
this world?*
We, like the Israelites want to be like everyone else.

It is not a popularity contest.

Samuel was a man who would not compromise his convictions.

I know so many religious leaders who are so easily persuaded in
their beliefs. They are easily prone to compromise their convictions.

They are more of a politician than a follower of God. In my
Christian life, I have sadly been acquainted with quite a few pay
check ministers.

It seems they have paper thin faith. Their convictions change
and diminish with the blow of a breeze.

Through all the religious experiences and hopping around, the
main result is more and more confusion and growing disillusionment
with God.

They are building their faith on falsehood.

The results are lives with no real substance or spiritual power.

*"Now listen to them; but warn them solemnly
and let them know what the king who will reign
over them will do." (1 Samuel 8:9, NIV)*

Samuel was a man of God!

He was called to warn the people.
We are called to warn others.
We are all called to be the watchmen-and-women of our time.
We all have the responsibility of the prophets.
Do you take this seriously?
Later in the scriptures:

> *Once again a message came to me from the Lord: "Son of man, give your people this message: 'When I bring an army against a country, the people of that land choose one of their own to be a watchman. When the watchman sees the enemy coming, he sounds the alarm to warn the people. (Ezekiel 33:1–6, NLT)*

This is for all who call themselves believers. We are all to be watchmen.

Do you warn others of the consequences of the actions of their lives?

How deeply are you involved in other's lives?

Are you aware through the scriptures the warnings of the Lord?

This is such a challenging and convicting verse.

> *Then if those who hear the alarm refuse to take action, it is their own fault if they die. They heard the alarm but ignored it, so the responsibility is theirs. If they had listened to the warning, they could have saved their lives. (Ezekiel 33:4-5, NLT)*

30

It is your call, as a follower of the Messiah, to be His messenger. Are you of the belief of "don't ask don't tell"? "Live and let live"? "No one's perfect"!

If so, you are unfit to serve the God of the scriptures. Remember the contrast in hearts. It gets dirty and uncomfortable.

> *But if the watchman sees the enemy coming and doesn't sound the alarm to warn the people,*

What if we do not follow and obey this verse?

> *he is responsible for their captivity.*

We are held accountable. What does that mean?

> *They will die in their sins, but I will hold the watchman responsible for their deaths.'*
> *(Ezekiel 33:6, NLT)*

This is something to consider if you call yourself a follower of the true way. Will you be a watchman or woman and confront sin and disobedience in others?

How does this compare with the present day leaders in all areas of our time?

1 Samuel 8:19–22 (New International Version)

Samuel warned them, they refused to listen to this man of God. They wanted a man as their king!

> *19 But the people refused to listen to Samuel. "No!" they said. "We want a king over us.*

> *20 Then we will be like all the other nations, with a king to lead us and to go out before us and fight our battles."*

Not much has changed in three thousand years.

We are to be set apart, different. It is our goal to embrace our separation from the world. We are called to be holy.

From the Old Covenant:

Leviticus 11: 45 New Century Version (NCV)

> **45 I am the LORD who brought you out of Egypt to be your God; you must be holy because I am holy.**

From the New Covenant:

> **Always live as God's holy people should, because God is the one who chose you, and he is holy. That's why the Scriptures say, "I am the holy God, and you must be holy too." (1 Peter 1:15–16, CEV)**

It is the same message in both the old and new covenants.

We are to be set apart.

We are to be of the same body and washed in the blood of the lamb.

The morality of the 'believer' of today deeply saddens and brings shame to God.

The hearts of the religious don't seem to change through the millennia.

> **21 When Samuel heard all that the people said, he repeated it before the Lord.**

Once again the blueprint for a spiritual person, go to the Lord, pray!
I am so impressed, inspired, and convicted by Samuel.
He loved the Lord! He wanted the Lord to be praised.
He allowed God to be God!

The theme of Samuel's life was obedience to his Lord.
How rare back then, and even more rare today.
Is your faith being added by your obedience?

If not, what is your faith built on?

> *22 The Lord answered, "Listen to them and give them a king."*
> *Then Samuel said to the men of Israel, "Everyone go back to his town."*

Saul: The People's Choice!

This is how the First King of Israel was decided!
Saul: the people's choice:
Remember, God is sovereign.
Either we are in His direct will, or in His allowed will!

It is so sad how people claiming to be of the Messiah live such sinful and worldly lives.

Their lives are filled with no power or true purpose. I know those who live lives of rules and obligations but no true inspiration from Hashem. It seems like their life is just a checklist. No feeling or inspiration behind it.

It is not easy to find true worshippers.

Samuel endured deep pain.

> *Saul was thirty years old when he became king, and he reigned over Israel forty-two years. (1 Samuel 13:1, NIV)*

Saul became the First King of Israel.
Samuel anointed him.
He was the people's choice for king. The Most High was rejected.
He would be what the people desired not God!
For the first time in the history of Israel, they had a king.

His name was Saul!

Who was Saul?

In the beginning Saul was a modest man from the tribe of Benjamin.

> **There was a man from the tribe of Benjamin named Kish. He was the son of Abiel, grandson of Zeror, great-grandson of Becorath, great-great-grandson of Aphiah—a Benjaminite of stalwart character. He had a son, Saul, a most handsome young man. There was none finer—he literally stood head and shoulders above the crowd! (1 Samuel 9: 1-2, MSG)**

He was the prototypical choice of the people.
He was the modern day leading man; tall, dark and handsome.
He was photogenic, and would look great on television.

Saul became the First King of Israel.
Samuel anointed him.
He was not the choice of God!

How often in business, sports, politics, and among the religious, does the rise of the "star" lead to corruption and devastation because outward appearance and the superficial are prominent? Inward character is often neglected.

We will see that over time the true heart of this man came to the forefront.

Saul lived a double life. As his role grew so did his pride and arrogance.

He was as the modern-day leader: one way in public, but entirely different in private.

There was no transparency or humility.

Saul was the people's choice.

He so well looked the part.

34

What grew in him over time was fear and insecurity.

From a personal view, in my walk with the Lord, I have encountered more than a few Saul's and sadly only a few Samuel's.

How about you?

Can you tell the difference?

What happened to the first king of Israel?

1 Samuel 13:13–14 (New International Version)

The people's choice for king was a constant thorn in the side of God, Samuel, and later in the side of David.

13 *"You acted foolishly," Samuel said.*

Foolishly, hmm!

> **You have not kept the command the Lord your God gave you; if you had, he would have established your kingdom over Israel for all time. 14 But now your kingdom will not endure;**

The promises of God are and have always been conditional!
Saul's kingdom would not endure.
Why?

He was not obedient.
What, you mean just believing is not enough?
No it is not!
Why?

> **the Lord has sought out a man after his own heart and appointed him leader of his people, because you have not kept the Lord's command."**

A man after his own heart!

The Most High desires men and women who seek after His own heart. How rare!

Is that how you want yourself to be thought of by God?

Or:

1 Samuel 15:10–11 (New International Version)

10 Then the word of the Lord came to Samuel:

Imagine God placing one of our names in place of Saul's. God was grieved. Place your name.

11 "I am grieved that I have made Saul king, because he has turned away from me and has not carried out my instructions." Samuel was troubled, and he cried out to the Lord all that night.

A pattern, Samuel prayed! Do we?

Take a moment to consider your own life. Are you living a double or even triple life?

Are you accountable and transparent?

If yes, to whom?

1 Samuel 15:17–26 (New International Version)

Samuel approached Saul:

17 Samuel said, "Although you were once small in your own eyes, did you not become the head

of the tribes of Israel? The Lord anointed you king over Israel. 18 And he sent you on a mission, saying, 'Go and completely destroy those wicked people, the Amalekites; make war on them until you have wiped them out.

Why was Saul rejected as king?

19 Why did you not obey the Lord? Why did you pounce on the plunder and do evil in the eyes of the Lord?"

Saul, like some we have known never got it.
For most it is never about the Lord!

Like today, it was about his following, his ministry, increasing his money, growing his power, and his personal Kingdom. Boy that is a lot of his.

He was fearful of what the people would think about him.

He was focused on the outward appearance. No transparency.

If this seems familiar, it is.

The modern leader is one of little substance.

He cared more about looking the part than having the right heart.

It is so hard to find a genuine humble hearted leader.

Unfortunately, this is all too common in the leadership of religion today.

Let's look at his response.

20 "But I did obey the Lord," Saul said. "I went on the mission the Lord assigned me. I completely destroyed the Amalekites and brought back Agag their king. 21 The soldiers took sheep and cattle from the plunder, the best of what was devoted to God, in order to sacrifice them to the Lord your God at Gilgal."

It was never his fault!

He was a modern-day politician. He did all he could to look good. He refused to be vulnerable. He could not be real.

He was consumed with the people's approval.

He lived a lie.

Like many religious leaders I have known these past few decades, Saul cared more about how he was viewed by man rather than God.

He was consumed by his reputation.

He was consumed with how he was viewed by men, but did not make an effort to be accepted by the most important observer: God.

He was unwilling to deal with the issues and moral wickedness of his heart.

It is amazing the common theme of the heart of the modern leader is "what is good for them".

They are all about their following, rather than following the Lord.

They do not care about those they are entrusted to serve.

The time came.

As it was his custom Samuel obeyed the Lord.

Saul was confronted.

> *22 But Samuel replied:*
> *"Does the Lord delight in burnt offerings and sacrifices*
> *as much as in obeying the voice of the Lord?*
> *To obey is better than sacrifice,*
> *and to heed is better than the fat of rams.*

We see here that the Most High desires obedience. This will be a continuing theme throughout this book, and with the deepest sincerity the scriptures.

> *23 For rebellion is like the sin of divination,*
> *and arrogance like the evil of idolatry.*
> *Because you have rejected the word of the Lord,*

he has rejected you as king."

God desires the heart that loves Him!
A heart that obeys His commands!

Remember, faith without obedience is nothing.

> **This is love for God: to obey his commands.**
> **And his commands are not burdensome. (1**
> **John 5:3, NIV)**

For you, the reader, here's a question to think about: how can you obey the commands of the scriptures if you do not know them?

How can we obey what we don't know?

We will look deeper into obedience later.

It seems that I have conversations daily with those claiming to have 'faith', yet are not knowledgeable of the book of life.

Please consider this:

> **Every word of God proves true.**
> **He is a shield to all who come to him for**
> **protection.**
> **Do not add to his words,**
> **or he may rebuke you and expose you as a liar.**
> **(Proverbs 30:5–6, NLT)**

In my writing and dealing with others this is a well-used verse.

The message from the Lord to the rejected king:

> **Because you have rejected the word of the Lord,**
> **he has rejected you as king." (1 Samuel 15:26,**
> **NIV)**

The challenge is to take these verses to heart in our own walk with the Most High. We are to acknowledge our failures and sins.

The Lord is pleased when we take responsibility and account-ability for our actions and decisions.

As we will see in the life of King David, he was motivated to please God. He would inquire of the Word and leading of the Lord.

Saul, on the other hand, was not concerned with the Word or leading from the Most High.

> *24 Then Saul said to Samuel, "I have sinned. I violated the Lord's command and your instruc-tions. I was afraid of the people and so I gave in to them.*

Remember Saul was the people's choice not God's.
Over one thousand years later, Paul declared:

> *Am I now trying to win the approval of men, or of God? Or am I trying to please men? If I were still trying to please men, I would not be a servant of Christ. (Galatians 1:10, NIV)*

This is our challenge.

It is so common, especially in the world of religion, to be obsessed with what other's think.

We so often crave, and are in desperate need of, the approval of men.

Look at this response by King Saul!

> *25 "Now I beg you, forgive my sin and come back with me, so that I may worship the Lord."*

Here again, he makes excuses and does not take responsibility for what he has done.
He wants this to be placed under the rug.
He fears the reaction of the people rather than the reaction of God!

26 But Samuel said to him, "I will not go back with you. You have rejected the word of the Lord, and the Lord has rejected you as king over Israel!"

He was rejected as king because he didn't obey God with a humble heart.
He had a rebellious heart filled with idolatry and pride.
Saul: the rejected king!

I remember when I was seeking to be trained to be a minister, my wife and I moved across the country simply by faith and seeking truth. We met with the main leader of the ministry, and he said something that is still stitched in my mind over a decade later. He said that the leaders I knew, and had problems with, will be elders or ministers for the rest of their lives, but be rejected by God. He compared these men with King Saul. This stuck with me.

Later, it was clear to me, that unless we deal with our hearts, we are all prone to being rejected by the Lord, although we claim to be of him. To my shame, I learnt this because it takes one to know one. I was the worst of the worst. I desired all that was just described. I desired the ministry, the position, the praise of man, and all the perks that came with it. To my shame, it took too long for me to figure out the obvious.

He was prophesying about himself. He was a real, modern-day Saul. He was consumed by his own agenda and position. He had a greater desire for the approval and praise from the crowd, then that of the Creator of the crowd. In all frankness, he was full of fear and undealt with hurt. Like Saul, he refused to take accountability for his actions and his sin. He, to this day, has the same bag of tricks that were old over twenty-five years ago. His faith, after almost a lifetime, has not grown.

Unfortunately, he attracted a plethora of Saul's. It was a ministry seeking power, not obedience.

I saw that that was the direction in which I was headed. I decided soon after that I wanted to be a spiritual leader like David or

Samuel, and not another Saul. It has been a long journey filled with pain, sorrow, rejection, great loss, and little fanfare.

But isn't that the road to the true kingdom of God?

The point to consider: how do you decipher between these two?

Looking at the previous scriptures, the main difference between Samuel and Saul was quite simple. This is the whole point of this chapter. Samuel was a man who deeply desired to follow, obey, honor, and please the Heavenly Father at any cost. It was not his aim or desire to fit God into his personal box. He made it his life's mission to fit into the plan of Hashem.

Saul, on the other hand, looked to have the favor of the people, and that meant looking good in their eyes. Following, obeying, honoring, and most assuredly pleasing God wasn't the aim of his heart. Saul looked to have God made in his image and his personal box, as most leaders in life do today. This is especially true in the religious realm.

In a sense, it was very much like today. The following was the most important element. Samuel had a very small following while Saul had a huge one. Samuel was a true prophet, Saul was a rejected king. Do the math!

What is the desire of your heart?

We will end the first chapter here and look at God's choice for his king in the next. We will examine the anointing of the next king, God's choice, David.

Before answering the chapter questions, please pray to the Mighty One to show you the state of your heart. Remember he cannot be fooled. He sees and knows all.

> ***Nothing in all the world can be hidden from God. Everything is clear and lies open before him, and to him we must explain the way we have lived. (Hebrews 4:13, NCV)***

It is time for you to reflect and examine your heart.

Chapter 1 Questions to Ponder

Please do not move forward until you ponder, seriously think through, pray through, and answer.

Remember the purpose of these questions is for you to begin dealing with your heart.

1. In your walk with God, how well do you know the scriptures?

2. How often do you devote time in the scriptures, daily, weekly, at all?

3. How do you view the differences between Samuel and Saul?

4. In your life, have you ever known a Samuel, a true godly man? Have you dealt with a Saul? When? How?

5. After reading this chapter, whom does your heart emulate more? Please ask someone close to you.

6. What is one thing, after reading this chapter, that needs to change in your walk with God?

MICHAEL P. WATERMAN

Answers to end of chapter questions

Chapter 2

The King No One Noticed

This chapter concludes the first sermon.

We ended the first chapter examining the rejection of Saul as the first king of Israel. He was not qualified to be the leader of Jehovah's people because he feared man and cared more about pleasing the crowd than the Lord.

We continue here looking at God's choice for the kingship of his flock.

David had so many talents. His harp playing and his Psalms stood out early in his life.

Let's look:

> *The Lord is my shepherd, I shall not be in want.*
>
> *He makes me lie down in green pastures,*
> *he leads me beside quiet waters,*
>
> *he restores my soul.*
> *He guides me in paths of righteousness*
> *for his name's sake.*
>
> *Even though I walk*
> *through the valley of the shadow of death,* [a]
> *I will fear no evil,*
> *for you are with me;*

your rod and your staff,
they comfort me.

You prepare a table before me
in the presence of my enemies.
You anoint my head with oil;
my cup overflows.

Surely goodness and love will follow me
all the days of my life,
and I will dwell in the house of the Lord
forever. (Psalm 23:1–6, NIV)

In the book of Psalms, we are able to see the heart of David. He was a true worshipper and a man who deeply loved and feared God.

David: God's Choice!

In this chapter, we will continue to see the heart of Samuel. He was a man of devotion and obedience to the Lord.

He was set to choose the replacement of King Saul, who had been rejected.

He was on a journey, unsure of his destination.

He was on this journey led by faith.

1 Samuel 16:1, 6–7, 11–23 (New International Version)

The main point of this lesson and the point of the Bible is that God always has a plan.

The question is will we trust Him and obey?

1 The Lord said to Samuel, "How long will you mourn for Saul, since I have rejected him as king over Israel? Fill your horn with oil and be on your way; I am sending you to Jesse of Bethlehem. I have chosen one of his sons to be king."

Samuel did! He obeyed!
He faithfully followed the Lord's call.

> **6 When they arrived, Samuel saw Eliab and thought, "Surely the Lord's anointed stands here before the Lord."**

Samuel was ready to anoint the next king of Israel.

Samuel served the Lord his whole life. He was a man God used powerfully.

Yet, like you and me, he was still a man.

It's funny he was about to choose another Saul, tall, dark, and handsome, but God:

> **7 But the Lord said to Samuel, "Do not consider his appearance or his height, for I have rejected him. The Lord does not look at the things man looks at. Man looks at the outward appearance, but the Lord looks at the heart."**

This is the point of the life of King David. Quite frankly, this is the point of our lives. No matter what we think, our most important quality is our hearts. This is what the Lord searches for.

David was not chosen because of his outward qualities or talents.

The God of Abraham, Isaac, and Israel chose this young shepherd as the leader of his people because of his heart's devotion.

It was his heart.

He saw inside the stuff of man he desired to lead his people.

None of the seven of Jesse's sons were chosen by the Lord.

Samuel was looking for a man. God wanted his man.

During this time, where was David?

One of the reasons David has had such an impact on my life is I can relate to him.

In my family, I am the youngest of three brothers. Growing up, I felt that I was the least. I was often sick. It seemed to me, I was the least impressive. The least talented, and had the least to offer. Like David, I was alone with the sheep. It seemed no one noticed.

Yet God would choose David, and he chose me to be the spiritual leader of the family.

Luckily:

God looks at the heart!

Not our appearance, intelligence, position in life, spiritual talents, our inner circle of influence, how we were raised, how much money we have, not the car we drive!

All of this is rubbish!

> **11 So he asked Jesse, "Are these all the sons you have?"**
>
> **"There is still the youngest," Jesse answered, "but he is tending the sheep."**
>
> **Samuel said, "Send for him; we will not sit down until he arrives."**

David was the youngest. The least impressive, he was not thought of highly enough by his father to even meet Samuel the prophet.

He was with the sheep.

Where did the Lord find us?

Samuel, as we have the opportunity to do, listened to the voice of the Lord.

It seems that we so often judge the physical, looks, talents, and abilities. It is so common to find ministries looking for a particular kind of person to lead.

They are seeking sharp, aggressive, but isn't it interesting that the heart is so often a non-factor? It isn't long before pride, arrogance, selfish ambition, and paranoia develop? The candidate, who sounded so good and had that look, turns into another modern-day Saul.

Samuel had to change his mind on the requirements and qualities the Lord desires.

He desires your heart.

He loves you more than you could ever imagine.

He could care less about what you look like, your race, what you do for a living, whether you are young or old, if you are married or have children, or any other criteria we focus so much on.

He is looking at the heart. The heart that only he sees when we think no one is looking.

Where do we fit in?

Consider the following:

> **Brothers, think of what you were when you were called. Not many of you were wise by human standards; not many were influential; not many were of noble birth. But God chose the foolish things of the world to shame the wise; God chose the weak things of the world to shame the strong. He chose the lowly things of this world and the despised things—and the things that are not— to nullify the things that are, so that no one may boast before him. It is because of him that you are in Christ Jesus, who has become for us wisdom from God—that is, our righteousness, holiness and redemption. Therefore, as it is written: "Let him who boasts boast in the Lord." (1 Corinthians 1:26–31, NIV)**

God chose you! Not man, but God, you are His!

How impressive were you when the Lord found you?

What were your spiritual credentials?
How grateful are you for his love?

How did God see David?

Let's go the Psalms.

> **He chose David his servant**
> **and took him from the sheep pens;**
>
> **from tending the sheep he brought him**
> **to be the shepherd of his people Jacob,**
> **of Israel his inheritance. (Psalm 78:70–72, NIV)**

He chose David because David was humble, a servant, a shepherd
of the sheep.
He was a man of integrity.

After spending many years looking through this man's life it is clear he learned how to be the king of the flock of Israel while no one watched. He guided smelly, stupid sheep as though they were the people of the Covenant. He played the harp, sang, wrote those incredible Psalms, and worshipped Jehovah all by himself.

He was being trained and prepared for the kingship while no one noticed.

He was more than willing to wait on the Lord.

His reality was guiding, shepherding, protecting, and providing for the sheep.

He learned that the Most High would always do the same for him.

Have we?

> **And David shepherded them with integrity of**
> **heart;**
> **with skillful hands he led them. (Psalm 78:72)**

David is anointed:

Let's go back to our main text:

> **So he sent and had him brought in. He was ruddy, with a fine appearance and handsome features.**
> **Then the Lord said, "Rise and anoint him; he is the one."**
> **So Samuel took the horn of oil and anointed him in the presence of his brothers, and from that day on the Spirit of the Lord came upon David in power. Samuel then went to Ramah. (1 Samuel 16:12–13)**

Saul had been the people's choice. God chose David to be the next king of Israel.

He was the man after the heart of God!

He was anointed with oil, and from that point on the spirit of the Lord was with him in power.

The only two people who had the Holy Spirit with them in the Bible before Pentecost for more than a brief period were John the Baptist and David!

Consider that for a moment. The Holy Spirit in the old covenant would be only a temporary thing. It would be, in a sense, being filled with the spirit. It was not indwelt with the spirit. It came and went.

With David, it was with him from the anointing of the oil until his last breath.

With the coming of the Messiah, his death at the cross, followed by his resurrection, and going back to heaven, it was to now be permanent.

As Peter preached the first sermon following the Messiah's ascension, it was declared.

> *"Repent," Peter said to them, "and be baptized,*
> *each of you, in the name of Jesus Christ for the*
> *forgiveness of your sins, and you will receive the*
> *gift of the Holy Spirit. (Acts 2:38, HCSB)*

What was the plan Hashem had for David?
This, my friends, is the heart of Jehovah.

> *Once, in a vision, you spoke*
> *to those who worship you.*
> *You said, "I have given strength to a warrior;*
> *I have raised up a young man from my people.*
> *I have found my servant David;*
> *I appointed him by pouring holy oil on him.*
> *I will steady him with my hand*
> *and strengthen him with my arm.*
>
> *No enemy will make him give forced payments,*
> *and wicked people will not defeat him.*
> *I will crush his enemies in front of him;*
> *I will defeat those who hate him.*
> *My loyalty and love will be with him.*
> *Through me he will be strong.*
> *I will give him power over the sea*
> *and control over the rivers.*
> *He will say to me, 'You are my father,*
> *my God, the Rock, my Savior.'*
> *I will make him my firstborn son,*
> *the greatest king on earth.*
> *My love will watch over him forever,*
> *and my agreement with him will never end.*
> *I will make his family continue,*
> *and his kingdom will last as long as the skies.*
> *(Psalm 89:19–29, NCV)*

What is his plan for you?

Imagine your name being there instead of David's. Compare that to the way God described grieving Saul.

Think about the Faith of young David and compare it to your faith, or if we are honest, our lack of faith. I am always humbled when considering this question. In all sincerity, sermons often come from the preacher preaching and convicting himself. The Holy Spirit is great at that.

David was a member of the Hebrews 11 hall of faith.

What is faith?

> *The fundamental fact of existence is that this trust in God, this faith, is the firm foundation under everything that makes life worth living. It's our handle on what we can't see. The act of faith is what distinguished our ancestors, set them above the crowd. (Hebrews 11:1–2, MSG)*

David was the Lord's choice for king. The reason was that he did all the work while no one noticed, or even cared to notice. The question to ask yourself, the reader; is what are you doing and whom are you serving when no one is around to notice? He sees and knows your true heart.

How does 1 Samuel 16 finish?

> *At that very moment the Spirit of GOD left Saul and in its place a black mood sent by GOD settled on him. He was terrified. (1 Samuel 16:14, MSG)*

Once the spirit of the Lord came upon David, it left Saul, and he received a different spirit. He was, from that moment, tormented with evil spirits for the rest of his life. He was a rejected king. He was in need of comfort.

Saul's advisors said, "This awful tormenting depression from God is making your life miserable. O Master, let us help. Let us look for someone who can play the harp. When the black mood from God moves in, he'll play his music and you'll feel better."

Saul told his servants, "Go ahead. Find me someone who can play well and bring him to me." (1 Samuel 16:15-17, MSG)

A major reality here is that God will use any quality, gift, ability, relationship in our lives to fulfill the purpose of his will. Nothing is trivial in our lives. There is no such thing as a coincidence. Remember, a theme I have had to continually learn, is that God's Will, timing, and purpose are perfect. Despite what I may think, he is never late. His timing is perfect!

Saul was in need of a harp player. David had been recommended to him.

One of the young men spoke up, "I know someone. I've seen him myself: the son of Jesse of Bethlehem, an excellent musician. He's also courageous, of age, well-spoken, and good-looking. And GOD is with him."

So Saul sent messengers to Jesse requesting, "Send your son David to me, the one who tends the sheep."

Jesse took a donkey, loaded it with a couple of loaves of bread, a flask of wine, and a young goat, and sent his son David with it to Saul. David came to Saul and stood before him. Saul liked him immediately and made him his right-hand man.

Saul sent word back to Jesse: "Thank you. David will stay here. He's just the one I was looking for. I'm very impressed by him."

> *After that, whenever the bad depression from God tormented Saul, David got out his harp and played. That would calm Saul down, and he would feel better as the moodiness lifted. (1 Samuel 16:18-23, MSG)*

Think about the irony here. The anointed king is set to serve and soothe the demons of the rejected king. This is how they met. If the Holy One can take a young shepherd boy no one cared to notice with a few sheep to serve the king, what do you think he has planned for you?

Trust that God always has a plan!

At a later time, describing the life and heart of King Saul:

> *So Saul died because he was unfaithful to the Lord. He failed to obey the Lord's command, and he even consulted a medium instead of asking the Lord for guidance. So the Lord killed him and turned the kingdom over to David son of Jesse. (1 Chronicles 10:13–14, NLT)*

This is why he was rejected by the Most High.

To close out this chapter:

> *Trust in the Lord and do good.*
> *Then you will live safely in the land and prosper.*
> *Take delight in the Lord,*
> *and he will give you your heart's desires.*
> *(Psalm 37:34, NLT)*

Take a moment and think about your heart's desire.

> *May the Lord answer you in times of trouble.*
> *May the God of Jacob protect you.*
> *May he send you help from his Temple*
> *and support you from Mount Zion.*

May he remember all your offerings
and accept all your sacrifices. Selah
May he give you what you want
and make all your plans succeed,
and we will shout for joy when you succeed,
and we will raise a flag in the name of our God.
May the Lord give you all that you ask for.
(Psalm 20:1–5, NCV)

Perhaps that opportunity or desire you have been praying and patiently waiting for is right around the corner. The question is: will you be able to recognize the Will of God because while alone you were being prepared?

Chapter 2 Questions to Ponder

1. Have you ever felt overlooked or ignored? How? What was the situation?

2. How do you view others? The outward qualities or their heart? How do you feel others view you?

3. What are you building your life on while unnoticed?

4. How do you feel God views you?

5. How do you view God?

Answers to end of chapter questions

Chapter 3

David and Goliath

We left the last chapter with Samuel anointing David to be the next king of Israel. We again took notice of the faith and obedience of the prophet Samuel.

This began the journey that David would endure on his road to the throne. It would be a long, lonely, and long-suffering time.

We ended last chapter with David playing his harp and soothing the evil spirits of the rejected king Saul.

This chapter is based on a sermon looking into the battle between David and Goliath. Please consider Goliath to be your greatest fear.

Fear, what a powerful one-syllable word. If we examine the effect that fear has on society, it would definitely baffle us. In the realm of religion, most, if not all, false teaching and hypocrisy stems from this word. Just take a moment and think about your life. How many bad decisions, lack of decisions, and regret came about from fear?

It is my challenge to you, the reader, to be real. This is the time where you are to get rid of the superficialities and shallowness so increasingly prevalent in this life.

What is your biggest fear?

Really, what is it?

Write it down.

We are going to continue our study in the life of King David.

We looked at the humble beginning of David. The youngest of eight sons, looked down upon, the least of his family. Left alone with those few sheep!

He was God's choice to be the next king of his people because he was a man after God's own heart.

To review:

In 1 Samuel 15, God rejects Saul as the king.

When we met David, he was with the sheep. After being anointed by the prophet Samuel (1 Samuel 16:13), he went back to be with the sheep. And in the end of 1 Samuel 16, we see an evil spirit begin to torment Saul. He is advised to have a musician play to soothe his torment, enter David, the musician. God will use whatever talent, experience we have to set us up for his will. That was how the next king (David) meets the rejected, current king (Saul).

Goliath: The Undefeatable Enemy

Our lessons in the life of David will continue as we look into the battle between David and Goliath!

What is your biggest struggle, fear? Your undefeatable enemy! Think about this!

What is your greatest fear?

What is a constant insecurity, weakness?

What keeps you up at night?

We are going to a battle that transpired over three thousand years ago. This will be the first time David is seen in public. It is his time to come on life's big stage of scripture.

He is going to see, hear, and feel the happenings of battle. What will he find?

He will find fear and witness faithlessness.

Let's go to the battle:

> **Now the Philistines gathered their forces for war and assembled at Socoh in Judah. They pitched camp at Ephes Dammim, between Socoh and Azekah. Saul and the Israelites assembled and camped in the Valley of Elah and drew up their battle line to meet the Philistines. The Philistines occupied one hill and the Israelites another, with the valley between them. (1 Samuel 17:1–58, NIV)**

There is a battle brewing between the Philistines and Israel.
The people of God against the enemy of God!
There has always and will always be a battle between good and evil.
The battle is between God and Satan and the battle is for ownership over our souls and our eternal destiny!

> **A champion named Goliath, who was from Gath, came out of the Philistine camp. He was over nine feet tall. He had a bronze helmet on his head and wore a coat of scale armor of bronze weighing five thousand shekels; on his legs he wore bronze greaves, and a bronze javelin was slung on his back. His spear shaft was like a weaver's rod, and its iron point weighed six hundred shekels. His shield bearer went ahead of him. (1 Samuel 17:4-7, NIV)**

Goliath is a frightening opponent!
He is a physical representation of our fear. He is an intimidating foe.

Think about how you react when confronted with that fear. How do you respond? Are you stuck in your tracks?

> *Goliath stood and shouted to the ranks of Israel, "Why do you come out and line up for battle? Am I not a Philistine, and are you not the servants of Saul? Choose a man and have him come down to me. If he is able to fight and kill me, we will become your subjects; but if I overcome him and kill him, you will become our subjects and serve us." Then the Philistine said, "This day I defy the ranks of Israel! Give me a man and let us fight each other." On hearing the Philistine's words, Saul and all the Israelites were dismayed and terrified. (1 Samuel 17:8-11, NIV)*

Goliath put fear and terror into the army of God!

What terrifies you? Please consider this.
How do you respond?
We so easily get caught in being paralyzed and stuck.

Goliath suggested that rather than the armies fighting, the battle should be decided by two men. Goliath (representing Satan) and a man from Israel (representing God)!

Isn't it interesting that this is the challenge? The "army of Israel" was paralyzed in fear because of the intimidating giant from Gath. He was a massive man. Imagine a huge offensive lineman picking a fight with you. It would seem unreal. His physical stature was indescribable. He brought great fear and terror into the "people of God."

The problem was no one was willing to face the enemy! He was to those present an undefeatable enemy! What is your invincible foe? Family, finances, health issues, character sins, relationships in the fellowship!

For many, the fear is to be alone. This fight would be one man against one man. The fates of two armies and two races of people would be won or lost as a result of the winner of this individual conflict.

A continuing reality in the word of God is that God has always and will always have a plan!

> **Now David was the son of an Ephrathite named Jesse, who was from Bethlehem in Judah. Jesse had eight sons, and in Saul's time he was old and well advanced in years. Jesse's three oldest sons had followed Saul to the war: The first-born was Eliab; the second, Abinadab; and the third, Shammah. David was the youngest. The three oldest followed Saul, but David went back and forth from Saul to tend his father's sheep at Bethlehem. (1 Samuel 17:12-15, NIV)**

The Lord orchestrated the arrival of David onto the scene. Remember David has never been a part of the army. He has never led men. He has spent his whole life away from the spotlight. He tended the sheep!
How about you?

> **For forty days the Philistine came forward every morning and evening and took his stand. (1 Samuel 17:16, NIV)**

Forty days. Not one, two, but forty days! Twice a day he would talk his trash!

This giant became a giant nuisance and a big problem for Israel. He kept coming closer and closer. The more time passed, the greater the terror became.

> **Now Jesse said to his son David, "Take this ephah of roasted grain and these ten loaves of bread for your brothers and hurry to their**

*camp. Take along these ten cheeses to the com-
mander of their unit. See how your brothers are and bring back some assurance from
them. They are with Saul and all the men of
Israel in the Valley of Elah, fighting against the
Philistines." (1 Samuel 17:17-19, NIV)*

*Jesse sent his youngest son to check in with his three older brothers.
What does the young shepherd find?*

*Early in the morning David left the flock with
a shepherd, loaded up and set out, as Jesse had
directed. He reached the camp as the army was
going out to its battle positions, shouting the
war cry. Israel and the Philistines were draw-
ing up their lines facing each other. David left
his things with the keeper of supplies, ran to
the battle lines and greeted his brothers. As he
was talking with them, Goliath, the Philistine
champion from Gath, stepped out from his
lines and shouted his usual defiance, and
David heard it. When the Israelites saw the
man, they all ran from him in great fear. (1
Samuel 17:20-24, NIV)*

*He is checking things out. His first taste, sight, feel, and hearing
the battle!*

I am sure he was disappointed with what he witnessed.
What does he witness?

David sees unnerving fear and unimaginable intimidation. He
arrives and, all of a sudden, finally there was a man of faith in this
army of fear. He was only observing at first.

They were terrified.

Think back to the previous questions pertaining to your personal fear. It is easy to relate to these men. They were not fit for the battle at hand. They were defeated spiritually and mentally before the battle even began.

Saul, if you remember was the leader of Israel, the King! He had been rejected. All he could do is offer bribes so someone else would fight the giant. It should have been him!

Remember, in the first chapter he stood above all the others in height. He was their king and leader. It was his role to fight for his people. The choice was for a king of flesh over the high all-powerful God. Israel desperately wanted to be like all the other nations. Sometimes you get what you ask for.

Who was Saul before God at this point?

He was the rejected king.

A thought to remember cowardly, rebellious leadership leads to cowardly, rebellious armies, families, businesses, and ministries!

We see it all the time, in all areas of life. In business, in politics, and unfortunately in the religious world, the wrong person is chosen to lead. The person might begin with pure motives, like Saul, but the road to the position is filled with compromise, corruption, and as a result, it undoubtedly leads to devastation. In my own experience, I have seen it too often in all areas of leadership. With greater influence and power, comes less and less accountability, and this leads to more and more deception, greed, and above all, pride. The position comes with it an appearance of integrity and character. Unfortunately, the person is rejected by the most important of all: God.

Are you a Saul? Becoming a Saul? Influenced by Saul's?

I know too many who are members of churches, work for bosses, and are involved with these types of leaders who are on their way to becoming just like how the Israelites are described.

They imitate their leaders. I also know wives living with abusive two-faced husbands, or vice versa. Their lives are filled with compromise, corruption, and are headed to destruction. There is so much anxiety.

Fear!

They are afraid to leave the situation. They feel they are without a choice.

How do I know? I was right there too. It is so easy to be influenced by corruption. It is like a frog in water. We are unaware that we are in the fire until it is too late. We become what we follow. We fall into the same tendencies. We are all of a sudden paralyzed.

What was Saul's ploy to avoid the personal battle?

> *Now the Israelites had been saying, "Do you see how this man keeps coming out? He comes out to defy Israel. The king will give great wealth to the man who kills him. He will also give him his daughter in marriage and will exempt his father's family from taxes in Israel." (1 Samuel 17:25, NIV)*

He, like our present-day corrupt leaders, used deceit, bribery, and money.

Here is a little secret I learned personally in a similar incident in my own life: a true follower of the Lord can't be bought off. I was offered a great opportunity in a Ministry in a great location — if I would only play the game. I would not play the game, and not surprisingly, did not get the opportunity. The saddest part is, the one who told me to play the game, was later treated harshly and let go of his position. In things involving the Lord, nothing is a game!

How about you, can your faith be bought?

What do I mean?

Are you willing to compromise your convictions for a job, money, a relationship, a position in a ministry?

At this point in his young life David's could not.

David: Faith Arrives on the Scene

For forty days, the armies are on opposite sides and Goliath draws nearer and nearer to Israel's side. He was talking trash. He was intimidating. The overwhelming response to fight him, one man of Israel and Goliath (the Philistine) was terror and fear!

Here came David! The man truly representing the Lord!

Now, finally, after forty days and forty nights, a true man of faith arrived. He would and could not be intimidated. He knew unswervingly who the true giant was.

> **David asked the men standing near him, "What will be done for the man who kills this Philistine and removes this disgrace from Israel? Who is this uncircumcised Philistine that he should defy the armies of the living God?" (1 Samuel 17:26, NIV)**

He didn't see Goliath as an invincible giant. He saw him as a disgrace to God! He was not intimidated by position, situation or title. All he saw was God! That is the first step to dealing with the Goliath's in our lives.

God is the true undefeatable, invincible all-powerful reality!

How do you see sin?

How about impurity, immorality, cheap grace, legalism, false teaching, double life, and lack of love?

David asked what the reward would be to defeat this uncircumcised pagan!

This can be you in your family, on your job, and in your fellowship. Let the Lord allow you to be known as a man or woman of faith and courage. You can be a majority for God all by yourself. You are never alone if you stand for the things of the Lord. It is time for the true leaders and worshippers to arise. We are living in a day where the Goliaths are spewing their threats. We, if we are to be his people, must be like David.

> *They repeated to him what they had been say-ing and told him, "This is what will be done for the man who kills him." (1 Samuel 17:27, NIV)*

Now, they are trying to bribe young David. Cowardly, rebel-lious corrupt leaders only multiply themselves.

Now this is family:

> *When Eliab, David's oldest brother, heard him speaking with the men, he burned with anger at him and asked, "Why have you come down here? And with whom did you leave those few sheep in the desert? I know how conceited you are and how wicked your heart is; you came down only to watch the battle." (1 Samuel 17:28, NIV)*

You can't, you are unworthy to be here! We know who you really are! If you remember Eliab was the most outwardly impressive of Jesse's sons. He could have fought too. He was afraid!

Eliab should have volunteered for the fight. He was afraid like the rest of the army, so he tried to make his little brother look bad to avoid his own fear. It is interesting that Eliab was not grateful for David bringing him food. He was just envious of the faith and cour-age exhibited by young David. The faithless and fearful will always have issues with those who are not intimidated or easily swayed.

They, deep down, wish they were the one to be filled with courage and bring faith.

> *"Now what have I done?" said David. "Can't I even speak?" He then turned away to someone else and brought up the same matter, and the men answered him as before. (1 Samuel 17:29-30, NIV)*

David was focused on who the real enemy was. Not his brother, the Philistines, the enemy of the Lord (Goliath).

He is only focused on the things of the Lord. He could have had several different reactions to the insults of his brother. He chose to overlook the faults of Eliab.

> *What David said was overheard and reported to Saul, and Saul sent for him. (1 Samuel 17:31, NIV)*

David attracted the attention of the king! No one else considered fighting this undefeatable enemy. They just accepted the challenge eighty times, twice a day for forty days!
He was not afraid. He offered hope in a hopeless situation!

The little brother, who was publicly insulted, suddenly became the only hope for the cowardly King Saul.

> *David said to Saul, "Let no one lose heart on account of this Philistine; your servant will go and fight him." (1 Samuel 17:32, NIV)*

He was not only ready, he was confident and bold. He knew something no one else there knew. He knew the power of the true God of Israel.

Again the voice of fear and lack of faith!

> **Saul replied, "You are not able to go out against this Philistine and fight him; you are only a boy, and he has been a fighting man from his youth." (1 Samuel 17:33, NIV)**

At first Saul tried to seem concerned about young David. Saul was focusing on fear, not faith. David knew who he was, and most importantly, who the Lord was.

This needs to be our response!

> **But David said to Saul, "Your servant has been keeping his father's sheep. When a lion or a bear came and carried off a sheep from the flock, I went after it, struck it and rescued the sheep from its mouth. When it turned on me, I seized it by its hair, struck it and killed it. (1 Samuel 17:34-35, NIV)**

He remembered past victories, the power of God in his life. David never thought he would lose. He knew it was God fighting for him! Do you?

Look at his boldness.

> **Your servant has killed both the lion and the bear; this uncircumcised Philistine will be like one of them, because he has defied the armies of the living God. (1 Samuel 17:36, NIV)**

Trials are an often occurrence in this life. We suffer and have difficult circumstances to deal with. We have battles. We, by faith, have miraculous victories to lean on when trouble comes knocking.

When the devil comes, overcome him with the past victories God has given you. Never forget!

It is interesting how we think our struggles are more severe than that of others. I know what you are thinking. I don't know the situation of your circumstances. I am not involved with your occupational hazards. I am not married to your wicked spouse. I am not responsible to pay your outrageous mortgage. I do not have to raise your children or deal with your aging elderly parents. The list goes on and on.

One thing to remember in this situation as Paul would pen later:

> *The only temptation that has come to you is that which everyone has. But you can trust God, who will not permit you to be tempted more than you can stand. But when you are tempted, he will also give you a way to escape so that you will be able to stand it. (1 Corinthians 10:13, NCV)*

One thing that has been helpful for me in times of difficulty and suffering is to remember times past where the Lord has delivered me through. Past victories in troubled times helps to build our faith for present and future trials. The victories are from above. We, on our own, are useless. The power is from Him! That is the key.

He continued to express his faith in the Most High.

> *The Lord who delivered me from the paw of the lion and the paw of the bear will deliver me from the hand of this Philistine." (1 Samuel 17:37)*

He had his confidence in the Lord! So should we, God is with us!

He had been trained for this time. He had been tried and tested as the shepherd of his little flock until the time where he would shepherd the flock of Israel. He was ready to seize his destiny.

Saul said to David, "Go, and the Lord be with you." (1 Samuel 17:37, NIV)

It is amazing how people try to sound spiritual despite where they are in their relationship with the Lord!

Take this event into proper perspective. In our life today, this seems like a movie. A little ruddy kid challenging a giant seems absurd. When you consider your "Goliath," now consider confronting it.

There are so many fears we have today. How am I going to pay this mortgage if I lose my job?

What if my worst fear comes true and my husband cheats on me?

How will I survive if something terrible happens to my children?

What if I get really sick?

What if I end up alone?

What if this boss from hell doesn't stop trying to push me to the edge?

How about in the religious realm, what will happen if I confront that leader's sin? How will I make it spiritually if I speak up against corruption in the eldership? How will I survive if I no longer have the crutch of the relationships in the church?

The fear questions can go on and on and on. With the questions come more fear and anxiety, not faith and hope.

Where in our thought process is the God of Abraham Isaac and Israel in these fear questions?

Remember the opposite of faith is fear. We are to live by faith.

In these verses of sacred scripture, all are consumed with fear and dread except one. They all have given up the hope of overcoming this invincible foe. The end looks bleak. They are the people of God. Like today, the majority of those who claim to be of the people of Jehovah are the same.

Are you one of the faithless many or are you the lone faithful overcomer? It is easy to say you are one of the few, but where do you stand with the fear questions? Or are you the David in your circle?

For so long, I consumed myself with what others thought. Are you like my sinful nature, wanting to be liked and accepted by all? Are you craving for the acceptance and approval of others?

If yes, it is a long, exhausting road that leads to nowhere. Do yourself a favor, and just deal with your heart. Please make it your goal to be one with the Lord; then find spiritual friends who are more concerned with your heart with the Lord than anything superficial.

The key to David, thus far in our study, is all that mattered to him was pleasing and being able to have the favor of his God. It was quite simple for him. He only concerned himself with what pleased the heart of his God. To him, Goliath was the puny kid and the Lord was the invincible giant.

A great thought process: there are many things that can overwhelm us, but it is all perspective. The fear is immense, but God is more. God is great. It truly is perspective.

Now we are about to see the continued contrasts between David and Saul.

Then Saul dressed David in his own tunic. He put a coat of armor on him and a bronze helmet on his head. David fastened on his sword over the tunic and tried walking around, because he was not used to them. (1 Samuel 17:38-39, NIV)

Saul tried to dress David as himself. Remember David had never been in battle.

He was told:

There was only one way to overcome the enemy, my way! Imagine it was a medium person wearing an XXL outfit. It looked and was ridiculous.

The faithless and corrupt are unable to solve serious issues. Often, they are living in what Einstein called insanity. They do the same things over and over, but expect different results. They do not want to admit their total lack of qualification for their position. They desire to look in control, when truly, they are faithless and full of fear. Sadly, once the trial arrives, they are shown to be greatly unqualified for their tightly gripped position.

What is the opposite of faith? Fear!

> *"I cannot go in these," he said to Saul, "because I am not used to them." So he took them off. (1 Samuel 17:39, NIV)*

David knew he only needed the Lord to help him!
Do we?

David was completely confident in his Lord. He put his money where his mouth was. He knew all he needed was faith. He was also an excellent shot. He was training for this moment though no one knew.

> *Then he took his staff in his hand, chose five smooth stones from the stream, put them in the pouch of his shepherd's bag and, with his sling in his hand, approached the Philistine. (1 Samuel 17:40, NIV)*

The battle that has been building up for forty days and forty nights was about to begin. There was Goliath, the giant from Gath, the undefeatable champion in one corner. On the other side David, a teenage shepherd of a small group of sheep. If this was a MMA fight, Goliath would be a ridiculously heavy favorite. Remember that, with God, all else seems small and powerless.

David: His Victory, a Victory for All Israel

The battle to decide master and slave is about to commence. Pay close attention this battle will not last long.

> *Meanwhile, the Philistine, with his shield bearer in front of him, kept coming closer to David. He looked David over and saw that he was only a boy, ruddy and handsome, and he despised him. He said to David, "Am I a dog, that you come at me with sticks?" And the Philistine cursed David by his gods. "Come here," he said, "and I'll give your flesh to the birds of the air and the beasts of the field!" (1 Samuel 17: 41-44, NIV)*

David was set for battle. Goliath tried to intimidate him. This time it didn't work! When we are focused on God, all else seems small. When we are focused on the problems and struggles, God seems small!

It must be odd for Goliath. He was used to being the ultimate example of intimidation. He was beyond a menacing opponent. He stared down this kid and attempted to strike fear and dread in David. He even begins talking the trash he had spewed the past 40 days. The scripture says he despised David. He cursed David. Did it work? Was the young son of Jesse struck with fear?

Let's go to the proverbial videotape.

> *David said to the Philistine, "You come against me with sword and spear and javelin, but I come against you in the name of the Lord Almighty,*

the God of the armies of Israel, whom you have defied. (1 Samuel 17:45, NIV)

For the first time in this battle, and maybe ever, Goliath was given a true reality test. He was the bigger, stronger and more experienced in battle, but it was not about that. What are our battles about? Who was Goliath really fighting?

Where is the war truly fought?

> *And that about wraps it up. God is strong, and he wants you strong. So take everything the Master has set out for you, well-made weapons of the best materials. And put them to use so you will be able to stand up to everything the Devil throws your way. This is no afternoon athletic contest that we'll walk away from and forget about in a couple of hours. This is for keeps, a life-or-death fight to the finish against the Devil and all his angels.*
>
> *Be prepared. You're up against far more than you can handle on your own. Take all the help you can get, every weapon God has issued, so that when it's all over but the shouting you'll still be on your feet. Truth, righteousness, peace, faith, and salvation are more than words. Learn how to apply them. You'll need them throughout your life. God's Word is an indispensable weapon. In the same way, prayer is essential in this ongoing warfare. Pray hard and long. Pray for your brothers and sisters. Keep your eyes open. Keep each other's spirits up so that no one falls behind or drops out. (Ephesians 6:10–18, MSG)*

This life is a spiritual battle. Most lose the battle before it even begins. Remember this chapter is about overcoming that great fear that keeps us from moving forward. The battle: Sales call, job interview, dealing with the boss from hell, the employee from hell, wicked account, your spouse, kids, parents, dreaded in laws, addictions, corrupt leadership in the fellowship, a slanderous friend, lingering bitterness, growing debt, the death of a loved one. Whatever it is, it is decided on your knees before it is even an issue. Don't underestimate the tuition, the daycare, rebellious friends, the upcoming terminal illness that will touch a loved or an accident. It is a War! A Spiritual War!

If you are not in the battle daily, in the Word of God, multiple times daily praying with intense desperation and truly living by a faith that is more than real, I am sorry to say, but you have already been defeated.

What was the young ruddy shepherd's response to the invincible opponent staring him down?

Back to our main text:

1 Samuel 17

I love this. This is how we are to confront our fears.

> **This day the Lord will hand you over to me, and I'll strike you down and cut off your head. Today I will give the carcasses of the Philistine army to the birds of the air and the beasts of the earth, and the whole world will know that there is a God in Israel. All those gathered here will know that it is not by sword or spear that the Lord saves; for the battle is the Lord's, and he will give all of you into our hands." (1 Samuel 17:46-47, NIV)**

David talks with confidence that the Lord will see him through! He knew who the real giant was!

You see, David was preparing for this opponent while no one noticed who or where he was. He knew the true undefeatable opponent, the high tower, and the stronghold of his soul: God!

He knew the true reality before it was penned by Paul:

> **What, then, shall we say in response to this? If God is for us, who can be against us? (ROMANS 8:31, NIV)**

Let's continue:

> **As the Philistine moved closer to attack him, David ran quickly toward the battle line to meet him. Reaching into his bag and taking out a stone, he slung it and struck the Philistine on the forehead. The stone sank into his forehead, and he fell facedown on the ground. (1 Samuel 17:48–49)**

One stone, down goes the giant!

It is like an overhyped boxing match or MMA fight. The fight is over before it even began. The saying is true, the bigger they are, the harder they fall. One stone was all it took to defeat the invincible foe. The same is true for us. It makes me think of times when dealing with religious bullies. One sentence or one question and they are figuratively knocked down. The battle was, is. and will always be the Lord's.

> **So David triumphed over the Philistine with a sling and a stone; without a sword in his hand he struck down the Philistine and killed him. (1 Samuel 17:50, NIV)**

David, due to his faith in the omnipotent God, triumphed. He brought a toothpick to a sword fight. A question to ponder; what if someone else fought Goliath? It would have been an ugly and different result.

Why you ask?

> *And it is impossible to please God without faith. Anyone who wants to come to him must believe that God exists and that he rewards those who sincerely seek him. (Hebrews 11:6, NLT)*

David took it a step further:

> *David ran and stood over him. He took hold of the Philistine's sword and drew it from the scabbard. After he killed him, he cut off his head with the sword. (1 Samuel 17:51)*

David did exactly what he said he would! He defeated the giant and cut his head off with the sword of the Philistine! What happened next?

> *When the Philistines saw that their hero was dead, they turned and ran. Then the men of Israel and Judah surged forward with a shout and pursued the Philistines to the entrance of Gath and to the gates of Ekron. Their dead were strewn along the Shaaraim road to Gath and Ekron. When the Israelites returned from chasing the Philistines, they plundered their camp. (1 Samuel 17:51-53, NIV)*

It was amazing, David defeated Goliath and the rest of Israel responded in kind. It went from fear and dread, to a victory for the entire army! We need to remember our past victories given by God!

Remember the results produced from following Saul? Never forget, corrupt, rebellious and fearful insecure leaders create corrupt, rebellious and fearful insecure families, businesses, governments, and most regrettably, ministries that keep God powerless and unable to truly bless.

On the other hand, the opposite is true. Faithful, obedient, prayerful leaders create God blessed families, businesses, governments, and most importantly, ministries that keep God powerful and able to truly bless.

This is a call to you. How will you lead?

Will you be a Saul or a David?

> *David took the Philistine's head and brought it to Jerusalem, and he put the Philistine's weapons in his own tent. (1 Samuel 17:54, NIV)*

David kept the weapons of Goliath and put it in his tent to remember the victory given to him by the Lord.

He kept the spoils of defeating Goliath as a reminder of the power of his almighty God.

> *As Saul watched David going out to meet the Philistine, he said to Abner, commander of the army, "Abner, whose son is that young man?" Abner replied, "As surely as you live, O king, I don't know." The king said, "Find out whose son this young man is." As soon as David returned from killing the Philistine, Abner took him and brought him before Saul, with David still holding the Philistine's head.*
>
> *"Whose son are you, young man?" Saul asked him.*
>
> *David said, "I am the son of your servant Jesse of Bethlehem." (1 Samuel 17:55-58, NIV)*

David went from the sheep to the limelight in one day. Only a man after God's heart could handle all the fame from killing the invincible giant from Gath!

When we truly live by faith, the Lord gives us more and we will be able to succeed because we give him the honor and the glory.

To close out this chapter, David goes from the shadows to the limelight in one day. His life would never be the same. He trusted in the one worthy of trust. He lived in a God-based reality and as a result; he overcame a foe that struck fear in the people of God. He, by faith, overcame fear!

This could be your name:

> **Whatever Saul sent him to do, David did it so successfully that Saul gave him a high rank in the army. This pleased all the people, and Saul's officers as well. (1 Samuel 18:5, NIV)**

We all have fears and battles. The question is, do we allow God to overcome our fear with faith and win the battles in prayer?

What is your Goliath or fear?

Is your faith in the all-powerful Hashem more than your fear?

For Saul, fear was the more powerful reality. He had to hide from the battle. For David, Jehovah was the only power. He fought and won and made it a victory for all Israel.

Will you live a life of fear or faith?

The choice is yours.

Chapter 3 Questions to Ponder

1. Please write down your biggest fear.

2. What is your Goliath?

3. When faced with this enemy, whom do you respond like? The Israelites or David?

4. What most impacted you about the role David played in the victory over Goliath?

5. What are you going to change as a result of this chapter to increase the strength of your faith?

Answers to end of chapter questions

Chapter 4

David and Saul

As we closed out the last chapter, we witnessed in scripture the coming on the scene for David, from the sheep pen to the battlefield. We saw how his faith in Jehovah led to victory for all of Israel. He was suddenly in the limelight. He was now noticed. He became a fixture in the kingship of Saul. After the victory over Goliath, David's life changed forever.

In scripture, Saul is an integral part throughout the early years of David's life,. We first saw in 1 Samuel 16, David comforting Saul with the harp. When viewing the lives and hearts of David and Saul after the victory over the Philistines, they demonstrate an incredible contrast of living by faith and living in fear.

In this chapter, we will see the fame and rise of David. He takes center stage in Israel's battles. At the same time, with this fame, there was a dark cloud brewing. In the life of David, it seems that there was a time for all seasons. This is certainly true when looking at the events that unraveled between David and Saul.

It was an interesting time in David's life.

His son Solomon would later add:

> *There is a time for everything,*
> *and everything on earth has its special season.*
> *There is a time to be born*
> *and a time to die.*
> *There is a time to plant*

and a time to pull up plants.
There is a time to kill
and a time to heal.
There is a time to destroy
and a time to build.
There is a time to cry
and a time to laugh.
There is a time to be sad
and a time to dance.
There is a time to throw away stones
and a time to gather them.
There is a time to hug
and a time not to hug.
There is a time to look for something
and a time to stop looking for it.
There is a time to keep things
and a time to throw things away.
There is a time to tear apart
and a time to sew together.
There is a time to be silent
and a time to speak.
There is a time to love
and a time to hate.
There is a time for war
and a time for peace. (Ecclesiastes 3:1–8, NCV)

We all experience different seasons in this journey we call life. If you are a true follower of the Messiah, the question to ask yourself is: what season are you in right now?

As the above scripture tells us, there are many seasons in this life. If you are a leader, what season are you experiencing?

At the close of 1 Samuel 17, we see David in a time of victory. He had just defeated the enemy in battle. With the victor, go the spoils. He is met by Saul, and all of a sudden, he is out of the shadows, and out for all to see. He is now a full-time leader in the army of Saul. The shepherd is now a warrior in the heart of the battle.

A good place to begin is right where we left last chapter:

When looking at the season, David was experiencing all was on the uptick. He was a man who it seemed could do no wrong.

> *Whatever Saul sent him to do, David did it so successfully [a] that Saul gave him a high rank in the army. This pleased all the people, and Saul's officers as well. (1 Samuel 18:5, NIV)*

Remember, God was with David. He did all well. His heart was focused on pleasing the Lord. All the people noticed the youngest son of Jesse. He had succeeded in winning the heart of all.

And all of sudden things changed.

> *As the troops were coming back, when David was returning from killing the Philistine, the women came out from all the cities of Israel to meet King Saul, singing and dancing with tambourines, with shouts of joy, and with three-stringed instruments. As they celebrated, the women sang:*
> *Saul has killed his thousands,*
> *but David his tens of thousands. (1 Samuel 18:6–7, HCSB)*

He was now held in higher esteem than the king, the rejected Saul.

This leads us to the beginning of the true training for the kingship David would endure. He has done nothing for his own benefit. He wholeheartedly served Saul, and aimed to bring honor and praise to Hashem.

When you consider the difficult times we experience in our lives, if we are honest, we are at least a partial cause.

What did David do to cause the ire and jealousy of Saul? Was he trying to steal the heart of the people from the king? Was he trying to oust Saul from the throne?

Was he a threat to Saul?

We would think Saul would appreciate David since Saul was saved from death. If Goliath would have defeated David; he would have killed Saul. The army of Saul was the victor due to the heroics of David. The people were in favor of the young champion. But:

> *The women's song upset Saul, and he became very angry. He thought, "The women say David has killed tens of thousands, but they say I have killed only thousands. The only thing left for him to have is the kingdom!" So Saul watched David closely from then on, because he was jealous. (1 Samuel 18:8–9, NCV)*

We must not forget that Saul was rejected as king and the spirit of the Lord had departed him. Here is where Saul begins to envy and fear David. For the rest of Saul's life, he is consumed with getting rid of the young shepherd. With this comes affliction and trouble for David. He is treated unfairly and has his motives clearly misjudged. Can you relate?

Let's clarify that David was not a threat to Saul. He was there to be a support and source of relief from the evil spirits tormenting King Saul. He was a champion for Saul. David had done nothing to bring about suspicion or paranoia from Saul. Saul's fear of David is not rational.

In my life, this has been a continual theme. Life is filled with the frustration of being misunderstood and wrongfully accused. It is interesting that in the realm of religion, if you are a true follower of the Messiah, life is eerily similar to the experience of David.

I think back to how naïve and zealous I was when I was young believer. I served the Lord and others wholeheartedly. It was great in the early years, because I excelled in blindly and foolishly following the orders of leaders. I was nothing near a threat for years. I was involved with the leader's families and took the appearance as reality. After experiencing a few seasons in this life, I grew up and became more knowledgeable of the Word of God and his Holy Spirit. I moved around a lot. Life was an adventure. I came back to where I was first converted, got married, and all of a sudden, I became aware of compromise and corruption in these leaders. I confronted them on it. It was not appreciated and it led to great pain over time. I was unable to deal with this reality, and like David, made bad decisions that lead to more pain and greater affliction. In retrospect, over a decade later, I was, in all honesty, not mature enough, either in life or spiritually, to undertake that conflict. Sadly, all it accomplished was damaging relationships. It began a long season for my journey that was filled with sadness and pain. The results led to a growing fear and insecurity in both myself and in the leaders I once had been very close to.

How about you?

Are you experiencing any mistreatment at work, at home, in school, or in your fellowship?

Do you have to deal with jealousy, gossip, slandering, or any misguided accusations? If so, consider yourself blessed.

Is your boss a tyrant? Do you have a harsh unloving spouse? A pastor who misunderstands you? If so, welcome to the true path to the Cross.

This is where my true spiritual journey to growth began. With rejection and mistreatment, comes a heart ready to understand the role that we are being trained for right now. Like David, the road is narrow and painful.

Peter would later author:

God will bless you, even if others treat you unfairly for being loyal to him. (1 Peter 2:19, CEV)

This is where the rug was pulled out from David. An idea that helps me when I am experiencing one of these trials, is looking in the scriptures and realizing that my troubles are nothing compared to what our spiritual forefathers endured. Perspective is very beneficial. Look at David's life here with Saul.

Forced to Flee

The next day an ugly mood was sent by God to afflict Saul, who became quite beside himself, raving. David played his harp, as he usually did at such times. Saul had a spear in his hand. Suddenly Saul threw the spear, thinking, "I'll nail David to the wall." David ducked, and the spear missed. This happened twice. (1 Samuel 10-11, MSG)

David knew of the evil torment Saul endured, and soothed him with the harp. Saul was not in his right mind. How else would he have not remembered young David between the end of 1 Samuel 16 and the beginning of chapter 17?

Think for a moment. Now imagine, you are at your office doing some paperwork, and all of a sudden, your boss comes in and throws a spear at you. His goal is to pin you to the wall. It seems so unreal. If you experience something close to this, I am deeply sorry. If you are going through any kind of abuse, imitate David and flee.

Saul was on the warpath.

Why?

Now Saul feared David. It was clear that GOD was with David and had left Saul. So, Saul got David out of his sight by making him an officer in the army. David was in combat frequently. Everything David did turned out well. Yes, GOD was with him. As Saul saw David becoming more successful, he himself grew more fearful. He could see the handwriting on the wall.

*But everyone else in Israel and Judah loved
David. They loved watching him in action. (1
Samuel 18:12-16, MSG)*

As a leader, isn't it common sense that when those we oversee are victorious, we are being successful? David as a leader in the army of Saul represented Saul. If anything, Saul should have rejoiced at the victory and success of David.

It is so simple. After being what surrounded by Saul's — the actions of Saul are clear. The rebellious, cowardly, and corrupt are easily given to be fearful once the opposite shows up. He saw clearly the words of Samuel coming to fruition in David, the "man after God's own heart." He knew that the next king, the choice of the Lord, was David. Truly understand that the opposite of faith is fear. This is the point where Saul considers David an enemy.

One might think well that Saul would have mentored David. He would do his best to set David up for victory. He would smooth the way for the kingship, God's choice to take the throne. What is ironic is Jonathan, Saul's son and the heir to the throne, did just that for David.

Saul, though, did all he could to keep David from the throne. Like modern church leaders, who know deep down that they not in line with the Will of God and are confronted with the heart that they need to emulate, do all in their power to hold on to their useless title. This fear of Saul is hidden from the people of Israel. I am always amazed how often that corrupt leadership, in any realm of life, is unknown to the majority of those represented. A friend of mine once described people as sheep. We smell, are dumb, and are easily deceived.

Again, if you are experiencing harsh treatment because of your faith, praise God.

Instead, Saul did all he could to appear like he embraced David. It was all a facade. He wanted David out of the picture.

Let's continue in 1 Samuel 18:17.

*One day, Saul said to David, "I am ready to
give you my older daughter, Merab, as your*

wife. But first you must prove yourself to be
a real warrior by fighting the Lord's battles."
For Saul thought, "I'll send him out against the
Philistines and let them kill him rather than
doing it myself." (1 Samuel 18:17, NLT)

This was so devious. Saul used David's humility, and the fact David was naïve, to set up his death. It is sad to see the plans of the evil one in action. He was bent on bringing David down.

Look at the heart of David. Like him, I can wholeheartedly understand what it is like to be taken advantage of and be used in the name of God. David felt all had his heart. He believed Saul had his best intentions in mind. He took Saul at his word. It seems, at first, he is unable to accept Saul's real intentions. I used to struggle personally, trying to understand the double lives and hypocrisy in business, and even more so in the family of the Most High.

How could God's ministers, eldership, and leadership groups be so corrupt and two-faced?

I realized that the heart of man is evil. I, over time, was forced to personally see the depths and wickedness of my own heart. The call of this book is for all to stop and deal with the fabric of our hearts.

It doesn't just happen. Often it begins with sincerity and a noble attitude. Over time, in order to grow and advance, it leads to compromising and taking short cuts. As a result, the core, or foundation, is not solid. It is like sand — easily shaken. That is where corruption develops. The saying is power corrupts; and absolute power corrupts absolutely. With compromise and corruption, unaccountability comes to lead to destruction. All of a sudden, the truth is revealed and no one can believe it. That is where we see Saul at this point in his life.

It, to my dismay, took me years to truly accept and finally leave. Oh, the naïve heart of young David.

The answer is because they, like me, are human. We all struggle mightily with sin. We all go through hardship. We all experience failure and heartache. We all go through seasons of defeat and sorrow. We all fail and fall.

The critical issue to consider is how will we respond?

The issue is how do we deal with it?

How do we deal with our heart?

The response of the youngest son of Jesse:

> *"Who am I, and what is my family in Israel that I should be the king's son-in-law?" David exclaimed. "My father's family is nothing!" So when the time came for Saul to give his daughter Merab in marriage to David, he gave her instead to Adriel, a man from Meholah. (1 Samuel 18:18-19, NLT)*

What a surprise a double-cross!

> *In the meantime, Saul's daughter Michal had fallen in love with David, and Saul was delighted when he heard about it. "Here's another chance to see him killed by the Philistines!" Saul said to himself. But to David he said, "Today you have a second chance to become my son-in-law!" (1 Samuel 18:20-21, NLT)*

Saul continued in his wickedness.

> *Then Saul told his men to say to David, "The king really likes you, and so do we. Why don't you accept the king's offer and become his son-in-law?"*
> *When Saul's men said these things to David, he replied, "How can a poor man from a humble family afford the bride price for the daughter of a king?" (1 Samuel 18:22-23, NLT)*

The earnestness of David:

> *When Saul's men reported this back to the king,*
> *he told them, "Tell David that all I want for the*
> *bride price is 100 Philistine foreskins! Vengeance*
> *on my enemies is all I really want." But what*
> *Saul had in mind was that David would be*
> *killed in the fight. (1 Samuel 18:24-25, NLT)*

He was setting up David to be killed by the enemy that David singlehandedly defeated for Israel. Remember this idea. It will come again later.

> *David was delighted to accept the offer. Before*
> *the time limit expired, he and his men went out*
> *and killed 200 Philistines. Then David ful-*
> *filled the king's requirement by presenting all*
> *their foreskins to him. So Saul gave his daugh-*
> *ter Michal to David to be his wife. (1 Samuel*
> *18:26-27, NLT)*

Think about this for a moment. Saul feared David and wanted him gone. What was the plan of Saul? It made no sense at all.

Well here enemy, take my daughter as your wife. We see that the cowardly and corrupt living in fear make terrible decisions.

> *When Saul realized that the Lord was with*
> *David and how much his daughter Michal*
> *loved him,*

Saul's daughter loved David. All of Israel considered David their hero. They all loved him.

> *Saul became even more afraid of him, and he*
> *remained David's enemy for the rest of his life.*
> *(1 Samuel 18:28-19, NLT)*

All loved him but Saul. To the Israelites:

> *Every time the commanders of the Philistines*
> *attacked, David was more successful against*
> *them than all the rest of Saul's officers. So*
> *David's name became very famous. (1 Samuel*
> *18:30, NLT)*

David did all right in the eyes of the Lord and the people. He was fighting the battle representing God.

> *War broke out again and David went out to*
> *fight Philistines. He beat them badly, and they*
> *ran for their lives. (1 Samuel 19:8–10, MSG)*

David lead the Israelite's to victory. He was the leader. He was being pruned and purified for the kingship.

What are you being pruned for?

> *This makes you very happy, even though now*
> *for a short time different kinds of troubles may*
> *make you sad. These troubles come to prove*
> *that your faith is pure. This purity of faith is*
> *worth more than gold, which can be proved to*
> *be pure by fire but will ruin. But the purity of*
> *your faith will bring you praise and glory and*
> *honor when Jesus Christ is shown to you. (1*
> *Peter 1:6–7, NCV)*

This period in the life of David helped create the king the people needed. In time, David would become a godly leader who endured trials and was able to see the clarity of the Lord.

The purification process is painful. It is needed to get all of the corrosion and impurities out of us, so our faith can be pure and real.

From the Limelight to No Light

This begins the season of David's life where he is truly trained for the kingship. The chosen king must suffer. And suffer he did. I once read that the Lord will not truly use someone until he breaks their heart. I have the scars to prove it, do you?

> *But then a black mood from God settled over Saul and took control of him. He was sitting at home, his spear in his hand, while David was playing music. Suddenly, Saul tried to skewer David with his spear, but David ducked. The spear stuck in the wall and David got away. It was night. (1 Samuel 19:9-10, MSG)*

A black mood from God! Saul was tormented by the Lord. Don't forget, he had been rejected as the king. David was the anointed one who had the spirit that the Lord had departed from Saul. Saul was more than aware of this. In essence, the reality is that from this point, and for the rest of his life, Saul was fighting not with man, but with God. Think about that.

This sets the stage for the season or time of being on the run and alone.

It sure didn't last long, did it?

We have seen David go from the sheep pen to the hero of the Lord's people. He had gained a prominent position in the king's army. He had gained a wife. He had the favor of all the people. He had it all!

Suddenly, out of what seemed nowhere, like a country music song, David had lost it all.

After protecting David from the wrath of her father, Michal resorted to lying due to fear. Like father like daughter.

> *"Why have you betrayed me like this and let my enemy escape?" Saul demanded of Michal.*

> *"I had to," Michal replied. "He threat-*
> *ened to kill me if I didn't help him." (1 Samuel*
> *19:17, NLT)*

Just like that the wife was gone. Their relationship unfortunately would never be the same.

> *So David escaped and went to Ramah to see*
> *Samuel, and he told him all that Saul had done*
> *to him. Then Samuel took David with him to*
> *live at Naioth. (1 Samuel 19:18, NLT)*

David was forced to flee for his life. The position in the king's
army was gone. The favor and support of the army were gone. His
relationship with Saul was never the same. As a result, he was on the
run for a long time.

> *My God, my God, why have You forsaken me?*
> *Why are You so far from my deliverance*
> *and from my words of groaning?*
> *My God, I cry by day, but You do not answer,*
> *by night, yet I have no rest. (Psalm 22:1–2,*
> *HCSB)*

Have you ever felt rejected by the Lord? David began a long
journey in which his heart was continually broken. He suffered much
rejection. He was, for the first time, taking his eyes of the master. He
was overwhelmed with fear, sadness, and discouragement.

Can you relate? He was on the run from an evil-spirited tormented hitman. The hitman's name was Saul, who happened to be
the king.

> *David went to see Ahimelech, a priest who*
> *lived in the town of Nob. Ahimelech was trem-*
> *bling with fear as he came out to meet David.*
> *"Why are you alone?" Ahimelech asked. "Why*

isn't anyone else with you?" (1 Samuel 21:1–9,
CEV)

He also lost his best friend: Saul's son, Jonathan. We will be looking at him later.

For now:

David was by himself and not acting like himself. He was very fearful. He went to the priests of the Lord.

> *"I'm on a mission for King Saul," David answered. "He ordered me not to tell anyone what the mission is all about, so I had my soldiers stay somewhere else. (1 Samuel 21:2, CEV)*

His fear leads to extreme consequences. He took his eyes off the Lord. The first problem, David lies. He compromised with the truth.

So often this is where most begin their fall from grace. We studied in the last chapter the power of fear. Fear can be an overwhelming enemy.

We see David here rather than seeking guidance and help from the Priests of Hashem, he lied.

The consequences were terribly tragic!

> *Do you have any food you can give me? Could you spare five loaves of bread?"*
>
> *"The only bread I have is the sacred bread," the priest told David. "You can have it if your soldiers didn't sleep with women last night."*
>
> *"Of course we didn't sleep with women," David answered. "I never let my men do that when we're on a mission. They have to be acceptable to worship God even when we're on a regular mission, and today we're on a special mission."*

> *The only bread the priest had was the*
> *sacred bread that he had taken from the place*
> *of worship after putting out the fresh loaves. So*
> *he gave it to David. (1 Samuel 21:3-6, CEV)*

He was hungry. He was all alone. He was running for his life. He was running from Saul. The thing was that other than a few, no one knew the young warrior was exiled. He was, for the first time, a man with his mind on all the problems and not on the true solution. He had lied to the priests. They knew him as Saul's best officer.

He compromised his convictions and faith.

> *It so happened that one of Saul's officers was*
> *there, worshiping the Lord that day. His name*
> *was Doeg the Edomite, and he was the strongest*
> *of Saul's shepherds. (1 Samuel 21:7, CEV)*

When we run in fear and lose sight of God, we resort to making bad choices. One of Saul's men was right there. This was to be a major regret of David.

> *David asked Ahimelech, "Do you have a spear*
> *or a sword? I had to leave so quickly on this*
> *mission for the king that I didn't bring along*
> *my sword or any other weapons."*
> *The priest answered, "The only sword*
> *here is the one that belonged to Goliath the*
> *Philistine. You were the one who killed him in*
> *Elah Valley, and so you can take his sword if*
> *you want to. It's wrapped in a cloth behind the*
> *statue."*
> *"It's the best sword there is," David said.*
> *"I'll take it!" (1 Samuel 21:8-9, CEV)*

He had no weapon. He took the sword that he received after he defeated Goliath. What a polar opposite exchange from when he first acquired the sword. Where did David go next?

> *That day David ran away from Saul and went to Achish king of Gath. But the servants of Achish said to him, "This is David, the king of the Israelites. He's the man they dance and sing about, saying:*
> > *Saul has killed thousands of his enemies, but David has killed tens of thousands.'"*
> *(1 Samuel 21:10–15, NCV)*

He went into enemy territory. He went to the people of Goliath. Why? Bad decisions lead to more bad decisions. He was led by fear. When fear is leading, it leads to much regret.

> *David paid attention to these words and was very much afraid of Achish king of Gath. (1 Samuel 21:12, NCV)*

The leaders were suspicious. Why would the warrior from Israel come to the enemy? They knew who David was.

> *So he pretended to be crazy in front of Achish and his servants. While he was with them, he acted like a madman and clawed on the doors of the gate and let spit run down his beard. (1 Samuel 21:13, NCV)*

He put on a show to make the enemy think he was crazy. It worked. I love the king's response.

> *Achish said to his servants, "Look at the man! He's crazy! Why do you bring him to me? I have enough madmen. I don't need you to bring him*

*__here to act like this in front of me! Don't let him
in my house!" (1 Samuel 21:14-15, NCV)__*

The old inmates run the asylum. Think about the actions of David. He had gone from being full of faith to full of fear. It can, and will, happen fast once our faith is replaced with fear. He had lost his mojo or swag. He had had a major change in focus.

Let's consider what we have read. He ran away from Saul to the priests. He lied to them. He then ran off to be with the enemy. He deceived them and fled once again. It seems he was a man without a people. He was the shepherd without any sheep. He was a leader of war missing an army.

His actions of compromise are leading to his corruption.

I can so relate to this point in the life of David. I was the golden boy in the church. I was close to many of the leaders. It was as if I was a member of their individual families. All seemed to love me. I could do no wrong. It seemed like I had so many friends. I was best man eight times in a matter of fifteen months. This was the case for years. All of a sudden, my eyes were opened to what was really going on in the ministry and in their personal lives. I soon confronted the sin. In my pride, and lack of true spiritual maturity, I came across as angry and condemning. It was a horrible job on my part. I was also bitter with what was taking place. I did not know how to process what was taking place. I was hurt and unable to handle the situation. I made bad decision after bad decision. This too, was the case for a few years. This was to my shame. Looking back, I responded like David with deceit and a lack of wisdom. It resulted in rejection, disillusionment, and great pain. In the wake of my journey, I hurt a lot of people. It could have been handled much differently. Thankfully, like David, I would get another chance, and that time, I handled it with faith and humility by the grace of the Most High.

It all happened so fast. David was reeling, trying to understand what had transpired. He was on the wave leading to greatness. He defeated Goliath, took the reign of the army, was given the king's daughter as his wife, had the love and respect of the people of Israel and was successful in all he did. He went from the sheep to the limelight, and as we will see in the upcoming chapter, to literally no light. Like the country music song; David lost his wife, job, friends, integrity, and his apparent sanity. The worst loss was coming. Saul would see to that.

How quickly our faith can turn to fear.

He was the man of faith in a faithless situation last chapter, and now he is a man full of fear.

It is amazing how quickly the seasons of life can change.

What season are you living in?

We will continue our study of David and Saul in the next chapter.

Please take your time with the chapter questions.

Chapter 4 Questions to Ponder

1. What season are you currently experiencing?

2. Have you ever had a Saul in your life?

3. Have you ever lost all it seemed? Lied? Went to the enemy?

4. How are you able to relate to David in this chapter? Saul?

5. Did you confront the sin in others? How did it go?

Answers to end of chapter questions

A LEADER'S CALL

Answers to end of chapter questions

Chapter 5

The Lonely Journey

Have you ever felt all alone? Really all alone!

As we closed out the last chapter, we looked at the walls closing in on David. He had gone from the limelight, a modern-day athlete or entertainer filled with the praise from all the people. He could do no wrong. He was the man who everyone wanted to be. He was the darling of Israel! In a lightning fast wave, his life began a downturn. He lost his position, his title, and his wife. He was a man on the run. He lost his grip on reality. He had been thrown a curve ball for sure. He was suddenly all alone.

We looked in the last chapter at David's plea. Read it out loud until you feel the despair.

> *My God, my God, why have You forsaken me?*
> *Why are You so far from my deliverance*
> *and from my words of groaning?*
> *My God, I cry by day, but You do not answer,*
> *by night, yet I have no rest. (Psalm 22:1–2,*
> *HCSB)*

For the first time in his life, he felt all alone. He felt deserted by the Lord. He was at a low point.

How do you respond to severe loss?

Think about your life.

You are let go from your company. Your wife says she is leaving. Your best friend betrays you. A loved one passes away. Your dreams are lost. How do you respond?

It is a difficult journey this thing we call life. It is filled with highs and lows. We all have victories and defeats. We all experience heartbreak. We are not shielded from pain. This is a good point to consider your life.

Are you able to relate with David?

I can so relate to where David found himself at this point of his life. He developed a faith in the Most High while no one cared to notice. He was so under appreciated by his family that he was an afterthought when the prophet Samuel arrived. He was looked down upon by his brothers. He made the best of what he was given. He led that little flock of sheep as though they were his children. He played the harp, sang songs, and protected them with his life.

I remind you of all this, to consider your background with the Lord. He worshipped and praised Jehovah all alone. He just wanted to serve the Lord. Then he was thrown into the mainstream world. All he did pleased Hashem. He excelled in this thing called life.

Take a moment to consider what you believe was the high point of your life. All was going well. The family was at peace. The ministry was growing. You felt you had true friends and healthy relationships. You were at the point in your career where it was a high wave of success. After being unnoticed, you are now in the limelight. For the first time in your life, you feel respected and appreciated. It is a time of feeling that you are in the Lord's favor. It was time to begin to upsize your life.

Then, all of a sudden, in what seems an instant, your mother is diagnosed with terminal cancer. The market crashes and now money is all but gone. The so-called friends and healthy relationships begin to decline and disappear. The ministry, that was growing, has been revealed as run by corrupt leadership. This begins a long time of suffering and pain. Over time, you become disillusioned with all you thought was true. You are left to think what happened? That is my story.

This is the point where we now find David. Like my experience, David found himself alone with time to regroup.

David: In the Cave

So David got away and escaped to the Cave of Adullam. He was in a smelly, dark and lonely cave. (1 Samuel 22:1–2, MSG)

He was all alone. He went from the sheep pens to fame, to being alone. He lost all his crutches. I am sure he had time to pray, think, and plan. He was learning a lesson.

I believe it is one of the hardest lessons to truly learn. He was learning to wait on the Lord. To trust and live by faith, though it seems all is lost. He was not going to quit. He would hold on to his Lord.

We get knocked down in life. The key is to not stay down, but to get back up. The key, for a true follower of the Most High, is to be able to take a proverbial punch.

King Solomon would later author:

Though a righteous man falls seven times,
he will get up,
*   but the wicked will stumble into ruin.*
(Proverbs 24:16, HCSB)

How do you respond when pain and suffering arrive? We are all knocked down. We all feel loss and defeat.

The question is how do we respond?

David would pen:

I truly believe
I will live to see the Lord's goodness.
Wait for the Lord's help.

> *Be strong and brave,*
> *and wait for the Lord's help. (Psalm 27:13–14,*
> *NCV)*

If you think about David's family dynamic, he was the over-looked son. At this time, Saul was a rejected king and as we will see a mad king as well. I am sure at this point Saul's rage and desire to kill David would affect his family.

We continue to *1 Samuel 22*:

> *1 When his brothers and others associated with his family heard where he was, they came down and joined him.*

He was alone trying to get his bearings and, all of a sudden, his family found him. His fall took him to a cave. A smelly and dark cave. There is more:

> *2 Not only that, but all who were down on their luck came around—losers and vagrants and misfits of all sorts. David became their leader. There were about four hundred in all.*

It seems that after biting his wounds and catching his breath, the Lord began to prepare him for the role of king. The troubled, indebted, and disheartened found David. It says down on their luck, losers, vagrants, and misfits. These men had no money, no hope, and pretty much were no good. They were looking for a new start, a new life, and a new leader. This motley crew in a cave, because of the Lord, would become the greatest army in Israel's history. They would be trained in battle, loyalty, and taught devotion to the Lord. Their leader, who kept them in line, was David. His heart remained soft to the Most High. God would turn lemons into lemonade. He was learning to be the king that the Lord desired. He was brought back to a familiar role as a shepherd over the sheep of Israel. When Samuel anointed him, he did not imagine that this was the way he would one day become king. I can relate to this.

I believe we are all able to relate with this. Think about where you are in life. Are you where you thought you would be?

What was your plan ten years ago?

Are you close to that plan? We think so differently than the Lord.

The truth about our thoughts and plans and those of Hashem:

> *The Lord says, "My thoughts are not like your*
> *thoughts.*
> *Your ways are not like my ways.*
> *Just as the heavens are higher than the earth,*
> *so are my ways higher than your ways*
> *and my thoughts higher than your thoughts.*
> *(Isaiah 55:9–10, NCV)*

Back to *1 Samuel 22:5*:

> *The prophet Gad told David, "Don't go back to*
> *the cave. Go to Judah." David did what he told*
> *him. He went to the forest of Hereth.*

He had a priest with him and, as we will see, he would be guided by God. He was now on the move. But this time, he had an army with him. Remember Saul was on the hunt for David. This was a consistent, wild goose chase for the rejected king.

> *Saul got word of the whereabouts of David and*
> *his men. He was sitting under the big oak on*
> *the hill at Gibeah at the time, spear in hand,*
> *holding court surrounded by his officials. He*
> *said, "Listen here, you Benjaminites! Don't*
> *think for a minute that you have any future*

with the son of Jesse! Do you think he's going to hand over choice land, give you all influential jobs? Think again. Here you are, conspiring against me, whispering behind my back—not one of you is man enough to tell me that my own son is making deals with the son of Jesse, not one of you who cares enough to tell me that my son has taken the side of this, this . . . outlaw!" (1 Samuel 22:6-8, MSG)

We are seeing David grow in his faith and trust in the Lord. On the opposite end, there was Saul. He was growing in his insecurity and fear. He was becoming more and more paranoid. He was desperate to see the end of David. He was using bribes and intimidation to find his enemy. The reality of the spiritual life: either we are growing or we are dying.

Where is your faith?

We ended the last chapter looking at David giving into fear and compromising his integrity by lying to the priests. There is an expression I like to use when talking with those who want to go out and make bad decisions. This is for believers and non-believers as well. I use this expression frequently. In reference to sin and the consequences it brings. Don't put more on your proverbial credit card then you are willing to pay.

Don't turn away so much that you will not be able to turn back to the Lord.

David is about to have his credit bill come due.

> *"They sow the wind
> and reap the whirlwind. (Hosea 8:7, NIV)*
>
> *Do not be deceived: God cannot be mocked. A man reaps what he sows. (Galatians 6:7, NIV)*

The consequences of our sins and bad decisions always arrive.

Saul: Growing in Madness

The bill always comes due!

> *Then Doeg the Edomite, who was standing*
> *with Saul's officials, spoke up: "I saw the son*
> *of Jesse meet with Ahimelech son of Ahitub, in*
> *Nob. I saw Ahimelech pray with him for GOD's*
> *guidance, give him food, and arm him with the*
> *sword of Goliath the Philistine." (1 Samuel*
> *22:9-10, MSG)*

Remember him from the last chapter. He was there to witness David. He tells Saul. There are always henchmen to corrupt leaders. These are those who are devoted to building their own position. They will do all to seem loyal. They are the kind who would sell out their own mother for personal gain. They do the dirty work. There are many like this in the 'church' culture. This man had no conscience before God.

> *Saul sent for the priest Ahimelech son of Ahitub,*
> *along with the whole family of priests at Nob.*
> *They all came to the king.*
> *Saul said, "You listen to me, son of Ahitub!"*
> *"Certainly, master," he said. (1 Samuel*
> *22:11-12, MSG)*

He had the priests, who had no clue about David being on the run, come to him, the king. They had no idea about what was going to transpire.

> *"Why have you ganged up against me with the*
> *son of Jesse, giving him bread and a sword, even*
> *praying with him for GOD's guidance, setting*
> *him up as an outlaw, out to get me?" (1 Samuel*
> *22:13, MSG)*

We see the growing case of mental illness in Saul. Remember, he was consumed with evil spirits. He accused the priests of God of betraying him. He became increasingly paranoid. He believed that all were against him. I know so many who believe this about their boss. Sadly, some feel this describes their spouse.

> *Ahimelech answered the king, "There's not an official in your administration as true to you as David, your own son-in-law and captain of your bodyguard. None more honorable either. Do you think that was the first time I prayed with him for God's guidance? Hardly! But don't accuse me of any wrongdoing, me or my family. I have no idea what you're trying to get at with this 'outlaw' talk." (1 Samuel 22:14-15, MSG)*

The priest tries to communicate the real situation. He defended the truth. The response of the rejected king:

> *The king said, "Death, Ahimelech! You're going to die—you and everyone in your family!" (1 Samuel 22:16, MSG)*

He commanded the death of the Lord's priests. He had lost all sense of right and wrong. He had no clue of reality.

> *The king ordered his henchmen, "Surround and kill the priests of GOD! They're hand in glove with David. They knew he was running away from me and didn't tell me." But the king's men wouldn't do it. They refused to lay a hand on the priests of GOD. (1 Samuel 22:17, MSG)*

He ordered his men to kill the Priests of the Most High! They refused. But guess who was more than willing to do the evil deed?

In the past few years, as I have begun writing, I have been enthralled by history. I watch the AHC channel. I have seen an inordinate amount of World War II documentaries. The overwhelming subject has been Adolf Hitler. It has been very interesting examining how and why he did what he did. The truth is, all of us are capable of great evil. If we allow fear and insecurity to lead to hatred and paranoia, then we are more than capable of great evil. This man allowed his mental illness to lead him to commit genocide. My point is, throughout his wicked and satanic reign, there were always henchmen willing to do his horrific deeds. This is Doeg. I have witnessed this in much lesser degrees in business and religion.

> *Then the king told Doeg, "You do it—massacre the priests!" Doeg the Edomite led the attack and slaughtered the priests, the eighty-five men who wore the sacred robes. He then carried the massacre into Nob, the city of priests, killing man and woman, child and baby, ox, donkey, and sheep—the works. (1 Samuel 22:18-19, MSG)*

Doeg killed them all, and all the people. It was a massacre. It was so not necessary. It was a bloody mess that should have never occurred. He killed innocent men, children, women, and animals. He killed his own people.

Why? That is what fearful, cowardly, and paranoid leaders do. They create terrible catastrophes. David's bill came due. His actions led to the death of all of these innocent people.

David Comforts

Only one son of Ahimelech son of Ahitub escaped:

Only one of God's priestly men survived. Where did this lone priest find refuge?

> *Abiathar. He got away and joined up with*
> *David. Abiathar reported to David that Saul*
> *had murdered the priests of GOD. (1 Samuel*
> *22:20-21, MSG)*

David was confronted with the tragic consequences of his actions. It resulted in the death of so many innocent people. Think about this. A lie leads to a massacre. All the priests of God were killed, but one. I couldn't imagine such an occurrence. Could you deal with all that death as a result of your actions?

Are you close to making a bad decision? Are you considering an affair? Are you on the cusp of taking advantage of someone in business? Are you entertaining following false doctrine that feeds into your sinful nature? Please consider the cost of these decisions. Are you able to handle the fallout? Will you be able to pay the bill?

What was the response of God's choice for the king?

> *David said to Abiathar, "I knew it—that day*
> *I saw Doeg the Edomite there, I knew he'd tell*
> *Saul. I'm to blame for the death of everyone in*
> *your father's family. (1 Samuel 22:22, MSG)*

He took responsibility for the consequences of his actions. We can see a growing contrast between David and Saul. He was now fully aware of the true extent of Saul's evil.

He had been in the cave alone with Jehovah. David, at this point, was back in his right mind. He saw his sin so clearly.

Do we? Do you?

I know so many who experience this type of life trauma. The main response is pointing fingers and giving responsibility to others. The issue is their hearts are like the one that Saul had. The point of this loss and pain is to bring us to an end of ourselves, and a humility that leads to repentance. So often, I see a pride and defensive attitude that leads to more suffering.

David took responsibility and humbled himself. He could move on. The goal is to move on, in peace and humility, with the Lord and others.

He comforts Abiathar. Imagine how he felt? All the other priests are gone. All the women, children, and animals were killed. He needed comfort. He fled for his life from Saul. He was now with the chosen king. David puts faith back in the priest.

> *Stay here with me. Don't be afraid. The one out*
> *to kill you is out to kill me, too. Stick with me.*
> *I'll protect you." (1 Samuel 22:23, MSG)*

He continued on the run, but had another priest added to his growing flock. He was the shepherd of this flock, and he would protect his sheep from the wicked wolf: Saul. The road to the throne would be long, winding, and twisting. He was forced to continually flee from Saul. Those he helped time and time again betrayed him, and he was a fugitive being hunted down by the rejected king.

In the next chapter, we going to change gears and examine the relationship between David and Jonathan, the son of Saul.

In our study thus far, we see the building of godly character and a soft heart in David. He is learning to truly live by faith and trust in God. He was being trained to be king by the King of kings.

In a sense, he was becoming the leader we are to strive to be.

What was David's heart toward Hashem at this point?

Psalm 18:1–3, 16–20, 28–36, 49–50 (NCV)

> *I love you, Lord. You are my strength.*

> *2 The Lord is my rock, my protection, my Savior.*
> *My God is my rock.*
> *I can run to him for safety.*

He is my shield and my saving strength, my defender.
3 I will call to the Lord, who is worthy of praise, and I will be saved from my enemies.

16 The Lord reached down from above and took me;
he pulled me from the deep water.
17 He saved me from my powerful enemies, from those who hated me, because they were too strong for me.
18 They attacked me at my time of trouble, but the Lord supported me.
19 He took me to a safe place.
Because he delights in me, he saved me.

20 The Lord spared me because I did what was right.
Because I have not done evil, he has rewarded me.

28 Lord, you give light to my lamp.
My God brightens the darkness around me.
29 With your help I can attack an army.
With God's help I can jump over a wall.

30 The ways of God are without fault.
The Lord's words are pure.
He is a shield to those who trust him.
31 Who is God? Only the Lord.
Who is the Rock? Only our God.
32 God is my protection.
He makes my way free from fault.
33 He makes me like a deer that does not stumble;
he helps me stand on the steep mountains.
34 He trains my hands for battle

so my arms can bend a bronze bow.
35 You protect me with your saving shield.
You support me with your right hand.
You have stooped to make me great.
36 You give me a better way to live,
so I live as you want me to.

49 So I will praise you, Lord, among the nations.
I will sing praises to your name.
50 The Lord gives great victories to his king.
He is loyal to his appointed king,
to David and his descendants forever.

This was written during his time on the run.

On the other side, we see the deterioration and weakening of a man's character. He was growing in fear, paranoia, and mental illness. He was losing his mind and on the way to losing his physical kingdom. He was a man rejected by God. This would be the growing story of Saul.

He was an example of the counterfeit leader, mentioned earlier. He is a warning of what not to be as a leader.

Which of these examples most describe you?

Chapter 5 Questions

1. Have you ever felt all alone rejected by all?

2. How did you deal with this?

3. Has your fear led others to suffer?

4. How do you respond to personal failure?

5. Do you know any Doeg's?

6. What is the main difference in David and Saul's hearts in this chapter?

7. Which one do you currently more emulate?

MICHAEL P. WATERMAN

Answers to end of chapter questions

Chapter 6

David and Jonathan

Jonathan: An Example of God's Grace

Moving forward with this chapter, after the last few, there will be a major change. Saul was a thorn in the side of David. He was led by jealousy, insecurity and fear. He hated David, and considered him to be his enemy. He was consumed with eliminating David from the situation. He only had his own ambition and desire in mind.

In the chapter after this one, we will see more of Saul. But for this chapter, we will be looking at a true friend.

What do you think about when you think about a true friend?

What is a friend?

Who is your best friend? Why?

In this chapter, we will examine the kind of friend we all should pray to be blessed enough to have, and more importantly, a friend we should pray to be for others.

In looking at the relationship between David and Saul, it is nice to shift gears to look at the kinship between David and Jonathan.

Who was Jonathan?

This is from a sermon I have preached.

Jonathan was an example of the comfort and grace God gave to David.
A godly friend!
Do you have a true godly friend?

Jonathan was the son of Saul. Imagine your best friend being the son of the man who has made it his mission in life to see your demise. The friend's sister was your wife, who betrays you out of fear for her father, your predator. How do they come into contact in the scriptures?

1 Samuel 18:1–4 (New International Version)

This takes place after David defeated Goliath, followed by a great triumph by the people of the Lord, Israel.

> *1 After David had finished talking with Saul,*
> *Jonathan became one in spirit with David, and*
> *he loved him as himself.*

This is an amazing man Jonathan the son of Saul.

Here we see a response to the heroics of David. We have looked at the fear and insecurity of Saul's response to David. In the response and attitude of Jonathan, we see one of connection and admiration. We see a desire to help and lift up. There was an immediate bond formed.

Have you ever just connected with someone where an immediate friendship was developed?

This is the relationship between David and Jonathan.

> *1 Jonathan became one in spirit with David,*
> *and he loved him as himself.*

He became one in spirit with David.
What does that mean?

120

To be one in spirit means to be like-minded and like-hearted. They had a similar thought process. Jonathan knew what David needed before David did.

He loved David as himself.
He gave all he had in order to help David.
Grace is a great indicator of Jesus love being in us.
How do we show love and grace to other's?

3 And Jonathan made a covenant with David because he loved him as himself

Jonathan made a covenant with David because of his love for him!

It is an incredible connection. There was a mutual respect and admiration for one another. Both were brave and courageous men. They both had a great faith in Jehovah. What a man of faith this son of Saul was.

4 Jonathan took off the robe he was wearing and gave it to David, along with his tunic, and even his sword, his bow and his belt.

Jonathan was the heir to the throne.
He gave all that signified his position to David.
How selfless!
He knew David would be the next king!
He sacrificed his entitled position for David!

It is as if he knew at the first meeting that David was the real king.

In the spiritual journey, we come across so many. There are all different kinds of people.

We worship in big groups. There are so many different personalities.

In a non-denominational fellowship, consider the different age groups, ethnicities, and cultures.

How often do we come across someone who sees our calling?

Better still, how many do all they can to help us reach that destiny?

In my life, it is amazing how, over time, connection can turn into insecurity and jealousy. It is so rare to find a true godly friend like Jonathan.

To find someone who is the heir apparent to our calling and voluntarily steps aside to allow us to grow into the position.

Please understand that if anyone should have feared the rise of the young shepherd, it was Jonathan. He was the heir to the throne of Israel. He was not concerned with any of that. He just felt moved to lower himself to the young warrior who defeated the powerful Goliath.

Later:

4 Jonathan said to David, "Whatever you want me to do, I'll do for you." (1 Samuel 20:5)

Let's review:

We looked at the evil Saul showed David, chasing him for years in order to kill him.

Jonathan was a friend.

He was the next to take the throne.

His father is David's enemy. He is in a very complicated position.

At this point, David is afraid that Saul wants him dead.

Jonathan assures him that he is okay.

David misses a holiday festival and asks Jonathan to find out Saul's true intentions.

They agree to meet a few days later, and the flight of an arrow would declare the fate of David.

If it was in front, all is well.

If it was behind, David would be on the run.

Jonathan pled with the king, his father on behalf of his spiritual brother, David.

He had sure found himself in a complex and difficult position. He made himself the voice or advocate for David. He placed his own position on the line. The verdict arrived.

Saul clearly made his intentions for David abundantly clear.

Saul revealed his anger and even flung an arrow at his son. David was to be killed.

1 Samuel 20:34–38, 41–42 (NIV)

The question was answered.

> **34 Jonathan got up from the table in fierce anger; on that second day of the month he did not eat, because he was grieved at his father's shameful treatment of David.**

What a tough situation to be in?

He had, in his heart, deep anger at his dad. He was clearly upset by the way Saul treated his friend. He was regretfully forced to be the one to confirm that David would be on the run for his life.

The day arrived:

> **35 In the morning Jonathan went out to the field for his meeting with David. He had a small boy with him, 36 and he said to the boy, "Run and find the arrows I shoot." As the boy ran, he shot an arrow beyond him. 37 When the boy came to the place where Jonathan's arrow had fallen, Jonathan called out after him, "Isn't the arrow beyond you?" 38 Then he shouted, "Hurry! Go quickly! Don't stop!"**

David's fears are true. He would have to flee and run from the king, Saul.

Jonathan let David know his fate. The arrow led to David fleeing.

He was a friend who told David the truth.

He was in a no win situation.

> **41 After the boy had gone, David got up from the south side of the stone and bowed down before Jonathan three times, with his face to the ground. Then they kissed each other and wept together—but David wept the most.**
>
> **42 Jonathan said to David, "Go in peace, for we have sworn friendship with each other in the name of the Lord, saying, 'The Lord is witness between you and me, and between your descendants and my descendants forever.' "Then David left, and Jonathan went back to the town.**

Jonathan did his best to encourage him!

They wept and said goodbye.

Jonathan went back home to his father who misunderstood and did not appreciate him.

David went into hiding.

Jonathan did his best to give hope to David. They wept. This was a heartfelt friendship. He was sad to see David go. He knew the tough terrain that David would have to endure. He made a vow to the next king, the choice of God to have friendship forever. He made David swear to remember him and once the time arrived of David's kingship to remember their friendship.

At a later time:

While David was at Horesh in the Desert of Ziph, he learned that Saul had come out to take his life. (1 Samuel 23:15–18, NIV)

David was himself during this period of his journey while running for his life. He had been constantly pursued and hunted by Saul. He was betrayed by those he protected.

Jonathan found David.

This was the last time they would meet here on this earth.
Again, David was on the run to save himself from Saul.

And Saul's son Jonathan went to David at Horesh and helped him find strength in God. (1 Samuel 23:16, NIV)

The constant pursuit and being on the run was getting to David. He needed comfort.

Jonathan helped David to find strength in the Lord.
Saul was trying to kill him, the enemy of God.
But Jonathan, the friend from the grace of God encouraged David, reminding him of the reality he lost.
God is, was and will forever be the true reality.

"Don't be afraid," he said. "My father Saul will not lay a hand on you. You will be king over Israel, and I will be second to you.
Even my father Saul knows this." (1 Samuel 23:17, NIV)

A godly friend brings us back to God.
What are the challenges we face:

Family issues, financial issues, relationship issues, addictions, just plain issues.

In preparing this lesson, it made me think about how important it is to have a real true friend.

I am grateful for the few real true godly friends I have.

I think back to something my father told me when I was young. He said that we should consider ourselves lucky to have one real friend. It is interesting that, when we are young, we think we will have many true friends. Unfortunately, he was right. When, as a young believer, I used to believe that I had many godly friends. It is sad to see that most disappeared when trouble came. Jonathan was an incredible contrast to his father. Saul's aim was to kill. Jonathan's aim was to love and build up.

What a rare quality.

Who is your Jonathan, strengthening you in the Lord today?

A better question, who do you help strengthen in the Lord?

The two of them made a covenant before the Lord. Then Jonathan went home, but David remained at Horesh. (1 Samuel 23:18, NIV)

This covenant David did not forget. He never forgot his best friend, Jonathan. A friend given by God!

That would be the last time the two met on this earth.

2 Samuel 1:26 (NIV)

I believe Jonathan was an incredibly loyal son to Saul. He died with him in battle (1 Samuel 31) and also an incredibly loyal friend to David. Think of how complicated that must have been.

After finding out about his death, as well as the death of his father, King Saul, David wrote this forever for all to see in the word of God!

Please feel the loss and sorrow in David's heart. He had seen the frailty of relationships in his young life. He had been betrayed by so many for whom he had put his life on the line. He was betrayed because of the fear others had of Saul. But David's friend Jonathan was loyal until his death.

> *I grieve for you, Jonathan my brother;*
> *you were very dear to me.*
> *Your love for me was wonderful,*
> *more wonderful than that of women. (2 Samuel*
> *1:26, NIV)*

After his friend's death, he remembered his love.

He remembered that during his time on the run God gave him a true friend, his name was Jonathan!

In our lives do we have a friend as loving and grace giving as Jonathan?

A better question, are we a friend like Jonathan?

The friendship of Jonathan is a great example of the friendship of the Messiah!

He made himself nothing so David could be king.

He showed David at a time when it seemed no one cared just how deeply God cared for him.

A thought to consider:

Without David, Jonathan would have been the next king.

Without Jonathan, David would have been killed!

Later, Solomon would pen:

> *A man of many companions may come to ruin,*
> *but there is a friend who sticks closer than a*
> *brother. (Proverbs 18:24, NIV)*

*As we look into the life of David the entire time we see God working.
We need to have the same heart of grace to all of the family of Jesus:
How do respond to the grace of God in our own lives?*

> **For Christ's love compels us, because we are
> convinced that one died for all, and therefore
> all died. (2 Corinthians 5:14, NIV)**

*To close out:
Please recognize that Jonathan is an old covenant story with new
covenant qualities.
Jonathan gave away all he had for David.
Remember:
David was a man after God's heart.
He was a shepherd, a harp player, a poet, a psalmist, a warrior, and
an incredible example of godly qualities.
David returned the grace shown to him.
He never forgot the grace Jonathan extended him.
He was forever changed from this friendship.
He gave back what he had been given!
But, Jesus:
What attracted Him to us?
What did He admire in us?
How did we encourage and inspire Him?
We didn't, we aren't we are nothing!
Jesus is the true example of grace.
Let's remember Him and extend grace to others the way we have
been extended!
While Jonathan was attracted to the qualities David possessed, God
loved us despite of who we are!*

> **But God demonstrates his own love for us in
> this: While we were still sinners, Christ died for
> us. (Romans 5:8, NIV)**

Jonathan gave up a lot for David. But Jesus died on the cross while we were still sinners!

It is quite a contrast examining the hearts of Saul and Jonathan. There could not be a more extreme difference. Saul lived in fear and was consumed with hatred. The son lived by faith and was consumed with love. In looking at the life of David, these are the two most significant relationships. One led by fear forced him to live by faith. The other led by love served as encouragement that David held onto the rest of his life.

Jonathan is the friend we all need to pray to have and also pray to be to others.

David would always know what it felt to have had a true friend. Do you?

Are you?

Chapter 6 Questions to Ponder

1. Do you have a true godly friend like Jonathan?

2. Are you a true godly friend like Jonathan?

3. What about the Messiah attracted you?

4. Are you aware of the grace and mercy you are shown?

5. Are you active in extending grace to others?

Answers to end of chapter questions

Chapter 7

The Predator Becomes the Prey

We return to the relationship between David and Saul. Last chapter, we examined the friendship between David and Saul's son Jonathan. It was a completely different dynamic. Where Saul felt fear and resentment towards David, Jonathan had a respect and admiration for the son of Jesse. Saul's life's ambition was to kill David. Jonathan made every effort to help his dear friend.

In this chapter, we will see a reversal of positions. David had the upper hand on Saul. He had the king in an extremely vulnerable position not once, but twice. This is a sermon I have preached to focus hearts on the act of forgiveness.

The goal is to forgive, and show kindness and grace to the undeserved. When we extend forgiveness, it shows our understanding that we have been forgiven for much worse actions. We are forced to look humbly at the cross.

We have looked at the cruel and evil treatment Saul had unleashed. He was a man set on murder. He was a king living in fear and torment. He had been rejected by the Almighty. He knew that David was God's choice to succeed him.

Let's look into the action.

David: Mercy to the Undeserved

The main point I want to emphasize is for us to strive for a heart that is filled with grace and mercy to those who have hurt, betrayed and sinned against us.

In 1 Samuel 19 David was forced to flee for his life because Saul wanted to kill him.

David fled and was on the run for a long time.

Why?

> **Saul was afraid of David, because the Lord was with David but had left Saul. (1 Samuel 18:12, NIV)**

We have looked at the journey David had taken. We are getting to the built-up confrontation that had to happen. In viewing this chapter, please examine your heart. The storm had been brewing. Saul had been on the hunt. He was about to encounter his prey, or so he thought.

1 Samuel 24:1–22 (NIV)

This will be the main text for this chapter.

What is happening?

Saul almost caught David in the previous chapter 23.

The Philistines attacked Israel so Saul had to go back and deal with the situation.

> **1 After Saul returned from pursuing the Philistines, he was told, "David is in the Desert of En Gedi." 2 So Saul took three thousand chosen men from all Israel and set out to look for David and his men near the Crags of the Wild Goats.**

He continued the pursuit for David who now has an army of his own.

But guess what happens?

> **3 He came to the sheep pens along the way; a cave was there, and Saul went in to relieve himself. David and his men were far back in the cave.**

Saul goes into a cave to relieve himself.

> **3 David and his men were far back in the cave.**

He went to the cave where David was hiding.

> **4 The men said, "This is the day the Lord spoke of when he said to you, 'I will give your enemy into your hands for you to deal with as you wish.'"**

His men who had been on the run with him try to persuade David to kill him.

David could take revenge!

These men wanted to receive the benefits of suffering with the next king!

What does David do?

What would you have done?

> **4 Then David crept up unnoticed and cut off a corner of Saul's robe.**

He cut the corner of his robe.

Let's think about this:

David had played the harp to relieve Saul, killed Goliath for the honor of God, Israel and the king, Saul.

He killed over a hundred Philistines for the price of marrying Saul's daughter, Michal.

He led part of the army of Saul with integrity.

He performed all with righteousness and wisdom.

Saul responded by taking away his wife, chasing him away from his position, killing eighty-five innocent priests and causing him to be on the run for more than ten years.

> **4 Then David crept up unnoticed and cut off a corner of Saul's robe.**

How would we respond?

How do we respond with one another, the attacks of family, coworkers, and the lost who bad mouth us?

How do we respond when our spiritual family attacks us?

> **5 Afterward, David was conscience-stricken for having cut off a corner of his robe. 6 He said to his men, "The Lord forbid that I should do such a thing to my master, the Lord's anointed, or lift my hand against him; for he is the anointed of the Lord."**
>
> **7 With these words David rebuked his men and did not allow them to attack Saul. And Saul left the cave and went his way.**

He was guilty!

What a heart for God.

He respected those who God allowed to be in positions of authority.

Not chosen, but allowed.

Do we?

The boss from hell!

The coworker who gossips and slanders!

The difficult spouse!
The brother or sister who betrays our confidence and hurts us in a severe way!
Belittling, labeling, slandering, wrongfully accusing!
How do we respond?

A better question is how should we respond?

From the mouth of the Messiah:

> **"You have heard that it was said, 'Love your neighbor and hate your enemy.' But I tell you: Love your enemies and pray for those who persecute you. (Matthew 5:43–44, NIV)**

This is a hard teaching!
Remember David was a man after God's heart, so humble!

1 Samuel 24:8–14

> **8 Then David went out of the cave and called out to Saul, "My Lord the king!" When Saul looked behind him, David bowed down and prostrated himself with his face to the ground.**

David confronted Saul!

> **9 He said to Saul, "Why do you listen when men say, 'David is bent on harming you'? 10 This day you have seen with your own eyes how the Lord delivered you into my hands in the cave. Some urged me to kill you, but I spared you; I said, 'I will not lift my hand against my master, because he is the Lord's anointed.'**

He showed Saul grace and mercy! Do we?

> **11 See, my father, look at this piece of your robe in my hand! I cut off the corner of your robe but did not kill you. Now understand and recognize that I am not guilty of wrongdoing or rebellion. I have not wronged you, but you are hunting me down to take my life.**

He went there!

> **12 May the Lord judge between you and me. And may the Lord avenge the wrongs you have done to me, but my hand will not touch you. 13 As the old saying goes, 'From evildoers come evil deeds,' so my hand will not touch you.**
>
> **14 "Against whom has the king of Israel come out? Whom are you pursuing? A dead dog? A flea? 15 May the Lord be our judge and decide between us. May he consider my cause and uphold it; may he vindicate me by delivering me from your hand."**

David was more than willing to let God judge between the two of them.

Is that your heart?

Paul later wrote:

> **Do not repay anyone evil for evil. Be careful to do what is right in the eyes of everybody. If it is possible, as far as it depends on you, live at peace with everyone. Do not take revenge, my friends, but leave room for God's wrath, for it is written: "It is mine to avenge; I will repay," says the Lord. On the contrary:**

"If your enemy is hungry, feed him;
if he is thirsty, give him something to drink.
In doing this, you will heap burning coals on
his head." Do not be overcome by evil, but over-
come evil with good. (Romans 12:17–21, NIV)

David understood the way of the Most High. He was well aware that the victory came from above. He allowed Jehovah to fight and win his battles. He knew that Saul's true enemy was the Lord himself.

He knew the Lord would deliver him. It is so sad how we are all prone to want revenge and take control. God is in control of all! David knew the Lord would be the one to defeat and handle the rejected king.

Our responsibility is to make every effort to live at peace with all. We are not responsible for other's action or reaction. This too is a hard and painful teaching.

David: Saul's Response to Grace

Saul responds:

When David finished saying this, Saul asked,
"Is that your voice, David my son?" And he
wept aloud. "You are more righteous than I,"
he said. "You have treated me well, but I have
treated you badly. (1 Samuel 24:16–17)

The grace and mercy of David moved the heart of Saul.
He had an evil spirit, but the grace of God awakened his heart.
How do we respond when someone we hurt shows us such grace and
mercy?

You have just now told me of the good you did
to me; the Lord delivered me into your hands,
but you did not kill me. When a man finds his
enemy, does he let him get away unharmed?

May the Lord reward you well for the way you treated me today. (1 Samuel 24:18-19, NIV)

We are grateful!
Saul reminds David of God's plan!
It makes me think about:
Later, Solomon, David's son wrote:

When a man's ways are pleasing to the Lord, he makes even his enemies live at peace with him. (Proverbs 16:7, NIV)

Saul continued:

I know that you will surely be king and that the kingdom of Israel will be established in your hands. (1 Samuel 24:20)

He asked a favor of David!

Now swear to me by the Lord that you will not cut off my descendants or wipe out my name from my father's family." (1 Samuel 24:21, NIV)

He wanted a very uncommon thing.
In the early eastern world, when a new kingdom took over, it was common to kill all the descendants of the former king!

So David gave his oath to Saul. Then Saul returned home, but David and his men went up to the stronghold. (1 Samuel 24:22, NIV)

David gave his oath!
A similar situation occurs in 1 Samuel 26, please read it on your own.

David on two separate occasions had the opportunity to kill Saul and take revenge for all of his wrongdoing. David instead displayed great mercy and undeserved kindness to the rejected king.

He even controlled the tempers of six hundred other men who wanted Saul dead.

What self-control.

The leadership of David taught six hundred merciless, graceless men the heart of God!

In looking at this chapter thus far, a question needs to be asked.

How would you respond if given a golden opportunity to seek revenge like David had?

Have you truly forgiven those who have hurt you?

Have you truly forgiven from the heart?

He wanted David to show him undeserved grace in the future.

This went against the custom of leaders.

In the eastern world, once a king was dethroned and replaced, the entire family would be killed.

I believe that Jonathan had a lot to do with the response of David:

> **I grieve for you, Jonathan my brother;**
> **you were very dear to me.**
> **Your love for me was wonderful,**
> **more wonderful than that of women. (2 Samuel**
> **1:26)**

He remembered what his dear friend said to him.

> **Jonathan said to David, "Go in peace, for we**
> **have sworn friendship with each other in the**
> **name of the Lord, saying, 'The Lord is witness**
> **between you and me, and between your descen-**

dants and my descendants forever.'" (1 Samuel 20:42)

David's Response:

So David promised, and Saul went home. David and his men returned to their hideout. (1 Samuel 24:22)

He promised to not forget the covenant to keep the line of Saul and Jonathan alive.

Later in his life, David remembered his friend. He would not forget the grace Jonathan showed to him.

David's response was similar to that of his greatest son, the Messiah:

At the cross:

Jesus said, "Father, forgive them, because they don't know what they are doing." (Luke 23:34, NCV)

There is an incredibly convicting verse about forgiveness.

We see that David forgave Saul after being chased and hunted for a long time by the crazed rejected king.

If we believe that we have been hurt or betrayed, and hold onto a grudge, then David's actions should convict us.

The key to forgiveness is remembering all we have been forgiven.

I recently spoke with a leader and elder, from the ministry I used to be a part of, about our time together. He and his wife have been a great help to my marriage. We spoke about a mutual friend going through a difficult time, and had been holding on to hurt from the past. I was convicted because it made me think back to when I was bitter, and hurt a lot of people. I remembered most how much I hurt him and his wife.

Once the Lord brought me back to my senses, I was broken. The brokenness led to godly sorrow and repentance. I apologized to all the people I had hurt. The last one was him. I was so embarrassed. We went to his house and talked. I remember feeling so uncomfortable at first. I apologized, and he set me free by saying those three magical words: "I forgive you". He had forgiven me long before we met. I was so relieved and joyful. Anyway, I reminded him of that and he made it seem like it never happened.

From that experience, how dare I not forgive others!

How about you?

Yes, if you forgive others for their sins, your Father in heaven will also forgive you for your sins. (Matthew 6:14–15, NCV)

In the great book, most of the promises of God are conditional. This is an example of that. Forgiveness is a salvation issue.

But if you don't forgive others, your Father in heaven will not forgive your sins. (Matthew 6:15, NCV)

If we are unwilling to forgive, we are unable to be forgiven.

Have you ever considered the ramifications of this verse?

In the next chapter, we are going to jump to a later time in David's life. He was the king of all Israel. God had given him all he had promised. He had been reminiscing about Jonathan in his heart.

David asked, "Is there anyone still left of the house of Saul to whom I can show kindness for Jonathan's sake?" (2 Samuel 9:1, NIV)

Jesus: Our Example of Mercy!

We have seen the heart of David!
Now we will look at the ultimate heart, that of Jesus!

> *Let us fix our eyes on Jesus, the author and per-*
> *fecter of our faith, who for the joy set before*
> *him endured the cross, scorning its shame, and*
> *sat down at the right hand of the throne of God.*
> *(Hebrews 12:2, NIV)*

We are to imitate David and fix our eyes on his greater son, our Lord Jesus.

He is:

> *the author and perfecter of our faith, who for*
> *the joy set before him endured the cross, scorn-*
> *ing its shame*

He joyfully took the punishment for our sin, the ultimate sign of forgiveness!

And like David:

> *and sat down at the right hand of the throne*
> *of God.*

He is with God!

1 Peter 2:21–24 (New International Version)

We are called to suffer:

> *21 To this you were called, because Christ suf-*
> *fered for you, leaving you an example, that you*
> *should follow in his steps.*

Jesus is the ultimate example:

> *22 "He committed no sin,*
> *and no deceit was found in his mouth." 23*
> *When they hurled their insults at him, he did*

not retaliate; when he suffered, he made no threats. Instead, he entrusted himself to him who judges justly. 24 He himself bore our sins in his body on the tree, so that we might die to sins and live for righteousness; by his wounds you have been healed.

We must do likewise!
Remember the true extent of suffering:

> *He was painfully abused,*
> *but he did not complain.*
> *He was silent like a lamb*
> *being led to the butcher,*
> *as quiet as a sheep*
> *having its wool cut off.*
> *He was condemned to death*
> *without a fair trial.*
> *Who could have imagined*
> *what would happen to him?*
> *His life was taken away*
> *because of the sinful things*
> *my people had done. He wasn't dishonest or violent,*
> *but he was buried in a tomb*
> *of cruel and rich people.*
> *The Lord decided his servant*
> *would suffer as a sacrifice*
> *to take away the sin*
> *and guilt of others.*
> *Now the servant will live*
> *to see his own descendants. He did everything the Lord had planned. (Isaiah 53:7–10, CEV)*

To summarize:

We must remember how important it is to show mercy and grace to others, especially if they have really hurt us or mistreated us!

It is an incredibly difficult thing to forgive. When our hearts have been deeply hurt, it is hard to move forward.

Are you holding back from forgiving someone? Are you unable to forgive yourself?

Are you holding a grudge against the Lord?

We looked at the verses. To be unwilling to forgive shows a true loss of gratitude.

When I am struggling with hurt, what helps me is to consider how much more my actions, thoughts, and words have hurt the Messiah. It is very helpful to remember that we have killed the son of God. It was our sin — our lack of forgiveness — that nailed him to the cross.

Please consider the end of chapter questions seriously before moving on.

Chapter 7 Questions to Ponder

1. How do you respond when someone close to you hurts you? Please give examples.

2. Do you seek revenge? Manipulate? Gossip? Please explain.

3. Is it difficult for you to forgive?

4. How would you have responded if you had the opportunity to seek vengeance like David did in 1 Samuel 24?

5. Are you able to connect to the cross for the ultimate forgiveness?

6. How do you respond to Matthew 6:14–15? Do you understand if you are not willing to forgive then you can't be forgiven?

7. What is one thing that you will change as a result of this chapter?

Answers to end of chapter questions

Chapter 8

David: Grace Remembered

In this chapter, we are going to a period much later in King David's life. We are skipping ahead many years. Consider it a flash-forward if you will. This is a good time to consider the time in his life where he was able to reflect.

We are at a time where the Lord had given his chosen servant what He had promised. He was, at this point of his life, the king of all Israel. He had the support of the people. He had acquired great wealth. It was at this time that the Lord had made Israel the envy of all other nations. He was now at a point where life had slowed down, and he had a chance to just reflect. He was reminiscing about his journey with Hashem, from tending the sheep to shepherding Israel. He had been given victory after victory. He had been reflecting, and Jonathan was on his heart. Jonathan had been gone for a long time, and he had a son alive but in hiding.

Let's go to the sermon.

David: Grace Remembered

2 Samuel 9:1–13 (NIV)

Let's realize this is an old covenant story with new covenant truth! David remembered. He never forgot about Jonathan or for that matter Saul.

148

At this point in his life, God had allowed David to be victorious in all he did.

He had complete military success.

He is at a time of peace and he has this thought.

1 David asked, "Is there anyone still left of the house of Saul to whom I can show kindness for Jonathan's sake?"

He desired to extend grace to a member of Jonathan's family.

What a thought, to extend kindness for past mercies given to us. David's life was a life nothing short of an adventure. He had spent most of his adult life in battle. He now had time to think and remember.

How often do we think about those who showed us grace at a time when we desperately needed it?

2 Now there was a servant of Saul's household named Ziba. They called him to appear before David, and the king said to him, "Are you Ziba?" "Your servant," he replied.

David does some research and finds a servant named Ziba from the house of Saul.

He asks:

3 The king asked, "Is there no one still left of the house of Saul to whom I can show God's kindness?"

Notice the response:

3 Ziba answered the king, "There is still a son of Jonathan; he is crippled in both feet."

He told David. There is, but he is crippled in both feet.
He is not attractive, sharp, he is needy. He is crippled!
You don't want him here!
How did this son of Jonathan become crippled?
Well:

> **(Jonathan son of Saul had a son who was lame**
> **in both feet. He was five years old when the news**
> **about Saul and Jonathan came from Jezreel. His**
> **nurse picked him up and fled, but as she hurried**
> **to leave, he fell and became crippled. His name**
> **was Mephibosheth.) (2 Samuel 4:4, NIV)**

He was dropped in haste because of the fear that David would kill
him.
Remember new regimes kill the old one!
David didn't care. He was just looking to extend grace to a relative
of his true godly friend.

> **4 "Where is he?" the king asked.**
> **Ziba answered, "He is at the house of**
> **Makir son of Ammiel in Lo Debar."**

Where?

He is in a dry unsettled land wasteland.
The bad part of town!
He was hidden for his safety.
Sound familiar!
It is like David when he was being chased by Saul, Mephiboseth's
grandfather.

> **5 So King David had him brought from Lo**
> **Debar, from the house of Makir son of Ammiel.**

David had him brought to him. Here we see the heart of God.

David wanted to meet and help his best friend's son.

> **6 When Mephibosheth son of Jonathan, the son of Saul, came to David, he bowed down to pay him honor.**
> **David said, "Mephibosheth!"**
> **"Your servant," he replied.**

Think about it, he was probably freaking out.
He had to be terrified.
He had spent his entire life hiding from David.
Now he was right before him.
He was most likely thinking it is over.

> **7 "Don't be afraid," David said to him, "for I will surely show you kindness for the sake of your father Jonathan. I will restore to you all the land that belonged to your grandfather Saul, and you will always eat at my table."**

But David was a man after God's heart.
He showed the son of his best friend the grace and unwarranted love that Jonathan and more importantly the Most High had shown him.
This is one of the best examples of the grace of God in the entire old covenant.
Consider:

> **and you will always eat at my table."**

Remember this statement!
He was overwhelmed, shocked.
I am sure David talked to him about the relationship he had shared with his father. I am sure they discussed his grandfather as well.

8 Mephibosheth bowed down and said, "What is your servant, that you should notice a dead dog like me?"

He felt so unworthy!

Wasn't it interesting that both young David and now the son of Jonathan have the same response to being included in the royal family?

9 Then the king summoned Ziba, Saul's servant, and said to him, "I have given your master's grandson everything that belonged to Saul and his family.

David restored the rightful inheritance to Mephibosheth.

This was the extension of grace we are to show one another. We are called to remember and hold dearly those who extended us the grace of the Most High. Here, David was bent on restoring the honor of Jonathan to his son.

10 You and your sons and your servants are to farm the land for him and bring in the crops, so that your master's grandson may be provided for. And Mephibosheth, grandson of your master, will always eat at my table." (Now Ziba had fifteen sons and twenty servants.)

He took care of those who would attend the son of Jonathan.
He lavished him.
To lavish means to give generously, plentiful, bountiful!
The love is similar to that of God:

1 What marvelous love the Father has extended to us! Just look at it—we're called children of

God! That's who we really are. (1 John 3:1, The Message)

Look at the marvelous love that God allows David to extend:

Then Ziba said to the king, "Your servant will do whatever my Lord the king commands his servant to do." So Mephibosheth ate at David's [a] table like one of the king's sons. (2 Samuel 9:11)

He became like one of the king's sons.
He would always eat at the table of the king!

In one day, he went from hiding from the king to eating at the king's table. He went from living in a barren land to living in the king's palace.

This could only happen by the grace and mercy of Hashem.

There is more:

Mephibosheth had a young son named Mica, and all the members of Ziba's household were servants of Mephibosheth.

He had a young son,

and all the members of Ziba's household were servants of Mephibosheth. (2 Samuel 9:12, NIV)

Talk about lavishing!

And Mephibosheth lived in Jerusalem, because he always ate at the king's table, and he was crippled in both feet.

He lived with David as a son, Mica as a grandson.

Just take a moment and consider this.
What favor and blessing!
Remember from this point forward:
For the son of Jonathan and the grandson of Saul:

he always ate at the king's table, and he was crippled in both feet. (2 Samuel 9:13, NIV)

He went from hiding in fear to being a part of the king's family where he ate at the king's table and I am sure that his crippled-feet were covered by the tablecloth.
All this happened because he was shown the grace of God by David! When David saw the son of Jonathan, he exhibited the heart of God:

Always remember how God chooses his special people.
It is not based on anything outward. He is unconcerned with our looks, talents, credentials, income, social groups.
What matters to Jehovah is:

The point in the scriptures we were first introduced to David.

**But the Lord said to Samuel, "Do not consider his appearance or his height, for I have rejected him. The Lord does not look at the things man looks at. Man looks at the outward appearance, but the Lord looks at the heart."
(1 Samuel 16:7)**

In the introduction, I wrote that David is my favorite biblical figure. This is one of the reasons why. He remembered the grace and mercy shown to him while he was at a low point in his life. He, at this point, was living in plenty and showers the crippled son of Jonathan with the grace and love he had not had. He could relate with Mephibosheth. He knew what it was like to live on the run for survival. He showed the mercy we are all extended now by Jesus.

Jesus: God's Love for Us

Before we close out, let's look at the ultimate example of grace.

I think another look at this verse is warranted.

Romans 5:6–8 (The Message)

Whenever we look at grace and mercy extended in the Bible we have to go back to the cross!
This is the ultimate example:

> **6 Christ arrives right on time to make this happen. He didn't, and doesn't, wait for us to get ready. He presented himself for this sacrificial death when we were far too weak and rebellious to do anything to get ourselves ready. And even if we hadn't been so weak, we wouldn't have known what to do anyway.**

How true this statement is!

> **7 We can understand someone dying for a person worth dying for, and we can understand how someone good and noble could inspire us to selfless sacrifice.**

This is the grace of David and Jonathan!
This is the heart of mutual love, admiration, and selfless sacrifice.
But the heart of God through Jesus is infinitely more:
Why?

8 But God put his love on the line for us by offering his Son in sacrificial death while we were of no use whatever to him.

To close out this chapter:

*Since you are precious and honored in my sight,
and because I love you,
    I will give men in exchange for you,
        and people in exchange for your life.
(Isaiah 43:4, NIV)*

Let us be imitators of Jesus love and give in exchange our own lives to allow others to feel the true love, mercy and grace of the Messiah.

In the end of the last chapter, I asked about your level of forgiveness. This chapter is a great example of forgiveness. If David had not forgiven Saul, after he himself experienced grace from the Lord, then he would have had no interest in extending mercy to Saul's grandson.

The reality is: if you are stuck holding grudges, you are unable to freely receive God's grace, and unable to give it to others.

In looking at David's life, he understood forgiveness.

Do you?

Chapter 8 Questions to Ponder

1. Is there anyone you are moved to show grace and mercy for the sake of the Lord?

2. Have you ever felt like a Mephibosheth?

3. How often do you take time to remember those who helped you when you were in need?

4. Do you realize how unworthy you are in relation to the cross?

5. How is your heart changed from this chapter?

MICHAEL P. WATERMAN

Answers to end of chapter questions

Chapter 9

David Turns Away from God

We took a detour in the last chapter, where we saw the built up and inevitable confrontation between David and Saul. All looked bright for the anointed chosen king. Let's review how God viewed this son of Jesse.

We saw this in an earlier chapter.

> *He chose David his servant*
> *and took him from the sheep pens;*
>
> *from tending the sheep he brought him*
> *to be the shepherd of his people Jacob,*
> *of Israel his inheritance.*
>
> *And David shepherded them with integrity of heart;*
> *with skillful hands he led them. (Psalm 78:70–72, NIV)*

What did God think of David?

> *Once you spoke in a vision,*
> *to your faithful people you said:*
> *"I have bestowed strength on a warrior;*

*I have exalted a young man from among the
people.*

*I have found David my servant;
with my sacred oil I have anointed him.*

*My hand will sustain him;
surely my arm will strengthen him.*

*No enemy will subject him to tribute;
no wicked man will oppress him.*

*I will crush his foes before him
and strike down his adversaries.*

*My faithful love will be with him,
and through my name his horn [a] will be exalted.*

*I will set his hand over the sea,
his right hand over the rivers.*

*He will call out to me, 'You are my Father,
my God, the Rock my Savior.' (Psalm 89:19–
26, NIV)*

The Lord found favor with David. He was the man after the heart of Yahweh.

So far, in our study of his life, David had had few lapses in his faith. Here he was at the point where the Kingdom was inevitable. Saul knew it. Jonathan knew it. All his men knew it. The people knew it. David was proverbially in the red zone, about to punch it in for the score, when he gave up. He was tired of running from Saul.

This is my favorite part of David's life. This is where we see his humanity and why it is so easy to relate with him.

This is one of my favorite sermons. It will be two chapters. The goal of these chapters is for you to examine your heart to see how fragile your faith is. In reality, we all turn away from the Lord a lot more than we would like to admit. We give in slowly, and then seemingly out of nowhere, the consequences show up. I remember when I first looked at this point of David's life. It was right after I was in a bad car crash. It was terrible. I was at a low point spiritually, and for the first time in my spiritual walk, felt all alone. I read a book about the life of King David. It really began to make me admire David.

In this sermon, I will review a lot of what we have already looked at. Please bear with me. Before you move forward, please pray for the spirit to show you where your heart is.

If you are not alert, your destruction could be right around the corner.

David: Turns Away from God

But David thought to himself, "One of these days I will be destroyed by the hand of Saul. The best thing I can do is to escape to the land of the Philistines. Then Saul will give up searching for me anywhere in Israel, and I will slip out of his hand." (1 Samuel 27:1–7, 12, NIV)

Saul was the king rejected by God in 1 Samuel 15. In 1 Samuel 16, David is anointed to be the next king. There is history between these two.

Whatever Saul sent him to do, David did it so successfully that Saul gave him a high rank in the army. This pleased all the people, and Saul's officers as well. (1 Samuel 18:5)

After serving Saul with his harp (1 Samuel 16 and 18), defeating Goliath (1 Samuel 17), leading in the army (1 Samuel 18), building a great friendship with Jonathan (1 Samuel 18, 20, 23), marrying Michael, the daughter of Saul (1 Samuel 18), fleeing for his life (1 Samuel 19–26), twice resisting the temptation to kill Saul (1 Samuel 24 and 26), and much more we come to this point.

After years of being chased by Saul, David had at this point had enough of bad leadership!
His first mistake,

But David thought to himself

Up to this point, David had inquired of the Lord. Here begins a sixteen-month period where he does not look to God!
We get in trouble when we think to ourselves without seeking the will of the Lord!

It is a bad sign when we start thinking to ourselves. We should pray to get the Lord's direction.

Are you growing tired with your unloving spouse, harsh, arrogant, unyielding boss, the kids constantly misbehaving, an old addiction coming back, or things just not changing in the ministry?

Are you tired of being single?

Do you deeply desire to be the bride and not a spectator?

Are you tired of waiting for that well-deserved promotion?

Are you and your spouse losing hope of getting pregnant?

This is where David finds himself.
What does he think?

"One of these days I will be destroyed by the hand of Saul.

Faithless! Been there!

We need to ask ourselves, where is our faith?

The best thing I can do is to escape to the land of the Philistines.

Who are the Philistines?
They are the enemy of the people of God! Goliath was a Philistine!

> **Then Saul will give up searching for me any-**
> **where in Israel, and I will slip out of his hand."**
> **(1 Samuel 27:1, NIV)**

He was so close to the kingship. This is a common theme for us, if we are honest. It is here we get the most impatient and disheartened.

This is where we take things into our own hands. We manipulate and, rather than speeding up the process, we suffer unnecessary pain and affliction.

Though at first:

He was right!
We continue:

> **So David and the six hundred men with him**
> **left and went over to Achish son of Maoch king**
> **of Gath. David and his men settled in Gath**
> **with Achish. Each man had his family with**
> **him, and David had his two wives: Ahinoam**
> **of Jezreel and Abigail of Carmel, the widow of**
> **Nabal. (1 Samuel 27:2-3, NIV)**

The result:

> **When Saul was told that David had fled to**
> **Gath, he no longer searched for him. (1 Samuel**
> **27:4, NIV)**

It was a break from the pressure. No more hiding. They had a time to chill and be relieved from the battle. If we are honest sin feels good at first. Think about our own lives:

After all, others do not know the terror of your spouse. The in laws and ill-behaved children. And dealing with your boss is just too much. The finances — oh don't get you started. The ministry is just too corrupt. Life is just too hard!

We all have pressures and stresses in this life. I know. It is tempting to just walk away. We walk away alright. We walk right into the devil's trap.

We feel so much better at first. The ability to walk away and just breathe seems priceless. Unfortunately, that is only the beginning.

I am sure most of the six hundred men were happy. A break, no more running for their lives.
I am sure that old bad habits came back.
It worked, right?

But at what cost?

Have you ever considered the progression of sin?

James 1:13–15 (New International Version)

13 When tempted, no one should say, "God is tempting me." For God cannot be tempted by evil, nor does he tempt anyone;

The key is to watch the progression. How do we sin in ways we never thought we would?

14 but each one is tempted when, by his own evil desire, he is dragged away and enticed.

Our own evil desire is where the fall begins.

15 Then, after desire has conceived, it gives birth to sin; and sin, when it is full-grown, gives birth to death.

The progression of sin: a thought that grows and leads to action and more action until we commit what seems the unthinkable.

I am of the belief that no one makes it their plan to become an alcoholic. No one desires to be an adulterer. It is nobody's dream to make a mess of their life and the lives of others.

Sin is not free! There is always a great cost!

We will more examine this progression in a later chapter.

*Back to **1 Samuel 27:6–7**.*

> **6 So on that day Achish gave him Ziklag, and it has belonged to the kings of Judah ever since. 7 David lived in Philistine territory a year and four months.**

A year and four months is sixteen months.

For sixteen months David lived with the enemy. Remember there were six hundred men and their families as well as David's two wives.

Our sin and bad judgement will affect others.

We think:

David was a man after the heart of God. He was the psalmist. He could survive spiritually in the land of the enemy. He would let his light shine! Satan wouldn't get to him!

In the next few verses (8–11) we see David living a lie. He was constantly lying to King Achish about his whereabouts and activities. He was living on the wrong side!

Ever been there?

Then:

> **Achish trusted David and said to himself, "He has become so odious to his people, the Israelites, that he will be my servant forever." (1 Samuel 27:12, NIV)**

What happened to the psalmist?

He became a great follower of the enemy. He was a man of intense passion, whatever he sought after he sought after with all his heart! I am like that! Good or bad!

Desire gives birth to sin and sin grows!

Let's move on to:

The Philistines gathered all their forces at Aphek, and Israel camped by the spring in Jezreel. (1 Samuel 29:1–5, 11, NIV)

There is going to be a battle. Whose side is David and his men fighting with?

As the Philistine rulers marched with their units of hundreds and thousands, David and his men were marching at the rear with Achish. (1 Samuel 29:2, NIV)

He is about to fight against his own people, the people who he will later lead. What happens?

The commanders of the Philistines asked, "What about these Hebrews?"

Achish replied, "Is this not David, who was an officer of Saul king of Israel? He has already been with me for over a year, and from the day he left Saul until now, I have found no fault in him."

But the Philistine commanders were angry with him and said, "Send the man back, that he may return to the place you assigned him. He must not go with us into battle, or he will turn against us during the fighting. How better could he regain his master's favor than

> *by taking the heads of our own men? Isn't this*
> *the David they sang about in their dances:*
>   *"'Saul has slain his thousands,*
>   *and David his tens of thousands'?" (1*
> *Samuel 29:3-4, NIV)*

The Lord intervenes! The Philistine leaders do not trust Him. It is amazing how when we are living a lie the truly worldly see right through us!

No one wanted David.

Ever feel that way? I have!

God worked to keep David from going to war against his own people.

> *So David and his men got up early in the morn-*
> *ing to go back to the land of the Philistines, and*
> *the Philistines went up to Jezreel. (1 Samuel*
> *29:11, NIV)*

They went back home!

What did they find?

> *David and his men reached Ziklag on the third*
> *day. Now the Amalekites had raided the Negev*
> *and Ziklag. They had attacked Ziklag and*
> *burned it, 2 and had taken captive the women*
> *and all who were in it, both young and old.*
> *They killed none of them, but carried them off*
> *as they went on their way.*
>   *When David and his men came to Ziklag,*
> *they found it destroyed by fire and their wives*
> *and sons and daughters taken captive. (1*
> *Samuel 30:1–6, NIV)*

The consequences of sin! All of their family, belongings, and territory burned. The response of David's men:

*So David and his men wept aloud until they
had no strength left to weep. David's two wives
had been captured—Ahinoam of Jezreel and
Abigail, the widow of Nabal of Carmel. (1
Samuel 30:4-5, NIV)*

They wept until they could weep no more. They saw the result of
their sin!

*David was greatly distressed because the men
were talking of stoning him; each one was bitter in spirit because of his sons and daughters.
(1 Samuel 30:6, NIV)*

It reached the point that his loyal men wanted to kill him. David
turned away from God!
The result, all was taken away.

*Then, after desire has conceived, it gives birth
to sin; and sin, when it is full-grown, gives birth
to death. (James 1:15)*

When we look at our lives this seems a little out of touch, really?

When we drift and turn away from God, there are always consequences. We lose our faith and live in fear. There is always damage.
In this example, David lost it all. First, he stopped inquiring of God.
He went to live in the land of the enemy. He became partners with
the enemy of God. He was not alone. He had six hundred men, their
wives, children, and all their belongings. He led his men straight to
the trap set by the devil.

Sadly, we do the same.

We think, it is only a drink, one cigarette, hit of pot, a little
porn, a little flirting, only one affair, a little doctoring of the books, a
little white lie. It goes on and on. We rationalize our bad judgement.
It feels good at first. But the bill always comes due. Are you willing
to lose it all for a moment of brief pleasure?

For David, it was all being taken away. During this time, he lost his wives, the families of his men, and all the plunder. It was all taken. The men wept uncontrollably and wanted to kill David. He had lost all.

Something happened:

David had been brought to an end of himself. He was about to be stoned by the sheep of misfits that the Lord had given him to shepherd.

It all became real, awfully quick. He came back to his senses. He remembered the Most High and turned back.

**But David found strength in the Lord his God.
(1 Samuel 30:6, NIV)**

Will you?

In the next chapter, we will see two things. We will see David turn back to God and truly repent, and we will see the grace of God who was getting David ready to sit on his throne.

For some of us, and some people we know, the consequences and bills of our sins keep coming due. The question is: what will it take for us to come back to our senses and turn back to the Most High?

He is waiting for us to find strength and hope in him.

Chapter 9 Questions to Ponder

1. Have you ever got tired of waiting for the Lord and took matters in your own hands? What happened?

2. Have you lost your faith and began living a carnal life? Please explain.

3. Have you caused damage to others and their families? What was the fallout?

4. Have you felt like God wasn't enough?

5. What did it take for you to come back to your senses?

6. How did the Lord help you overcome?

A LEADER'S CALL

Answers to end of chapter questions

A LEADER'S CALL

Answers to end of chapter questions

Chapter 10

David Turns Back to God

It is not difficult. In fact, turning away from the Lord can be quite easy. It all begins by losing hope and focusing on the things we do not see happening. We are so easily distracted by the things in this life. We are so prone to missing the mark.

If we have a faith in the Most High, the enemy of our souls will be out to get us. He is on a mission to steal our joy. I am referring to that voice inside our head that says we will never fulfill our dreams and that the Lord is not on our side. We all have things we are trying to overcome, and by faith, we persevere. The devil is telling us all that it takes to deter us and lead us to compromise, corruption, and ultimately, to our destruction.

The Apostle Peter declared,

> *Be serious! Be alert! Your adversary the Devil*
> *is prowling around like a roaring lion, looking*
> *for anyone he can devour. (1 Peter 5:8, HCSB)*

We are to push forward and not give up. In the last chapter, I shared how David was so close to achieving his desire, and the promises and blessings of Hashem. He let the enemy deter him from enduring and receiving the victory.

The bills came due. He was unable to deal with the consequences of his sin, and lost hope. It is key to consider that this can happen to us if we are not careful. Please make it a habit to consider the cost of your bad decisions. The bill is always close to coming due.

This is an incredibly challenging, yet inspiring and encouraging, chapter. We left off last chapter, looking at what appeared to be the end for David. His men were so brokenhearted by the loss of their families that they wanted to stone David to death. This is what woke him from his sixteen-month spiritual slumber.

He turned back to God and he recovered all. He began inquiring of the Lord and had his faith in Hashem restored. He then showed why he was the choice for the king.

David: Turns Back to God

> **But David found strength in the Lord his God.**
> **(1 Samuel 30)**

David was back!

He regained his faith. He recovered his reverence and awe of the Most High. He went back to the real source of his strength and the true giver of victory. His eyes were not blinded by the lust of sin. He was back in his walk with God!

> **Then David said to Abiathar the priest, the son**
> **of Ahimelech, "Bring me the ephod." Abiathar**
> **brought it to him, and David inquired of the**
> **Lord, "Shall I pursue this raiding party? Will I**
> **overtake them?" (1 Samuel 30:7-8, NIV)**

He inquired of the Lord! For the first time in sixteen months David sought God!

The ephod was the will of God. It was a breastplate which the priests would wear. When inquiring of the Lord, the answer was no if it remained dim, and yes if it was bright.

"Pursue them," he answered. "You will certainly overtake them and succeed in the rescue." (1 Samuel 30:8, NIV)

The grace of our heavenly father!

Just like that he was forgiven.

David and the six hundred men with him came to the Besor Ravine, where some stayed behind,

David was fired up!
All of a sudden, he was back to being the faithful shepherd of Israel!
Check this out!

This is why I love this portion of scripture.

for two hundred men were too exhausted to cross the ravine. But David and four hundred men continued the pursuit. (1 Samuel 30:9-10, NIV)

They could not keep up with him! He was crawling in sin with them and now he is running ahead with the Lord!
David found an Egyptian slave who was abandoned by an Amalekite. He led David and his men to their families.

He led David down, and there they were, scattered over the countryside, eating, drinking and reveling because of the great amount of plunder they had taken from the land of the Philistines and from Judah. (1 Samuel 30:16, NIV)

They were celebrating their short-term victory.
But remember, David was a man after the heart of God!

> *David fought them from dusk until the evening*
> *of the next day, and none of them got away,*
> *except four hundred young men who rode off*
> *on camels and fled. (1 Samuel 30:17, NIV)*

Wow!
The result:

> *David recovered everything the Amalekites had*
> *taken, including his two wives. Nothing was*
> *missing: young or old, boy or girl, plunder or*
> *anything else they had taken. David brought*
> *everything back. He took all the flocks and*
> *herds, and his men drove them ahead of the*
> *other livestock, saying, "This is David's plun-*
> *der." (1 Samuel 30:18-20, NIV)*
> *David recovered everything!*

He turned back to God!

He was now living and surging forward with the Lord leading every step he took. He was the chosen vessel for the king of the Lord's people. He lost his focus, and ran to the side of the enemy, but he was brought back to his calling to be the greatest king in the history of the world. He did not turn so far away from the Most High that he couldn't turn back.

Have we?

This book is written to help the reader examine their faith. Where is it? In looking at the life of David, it is impossible to not see the need to deal with our hearts. David lost all and, in desperation, found strength in the Lord. This is a road map for us. David spent sixteen long months leading his men into darkness. He led them to compromise, corruption, and to the precipice of destruction.

As a result of this compromise, the bill came due. He was held responsible by his men for their families being taken away. They wept and wept, and in turn, came to the conclusion to stone David,. What did he do to turn things around?

Did he come up with a plan to manipulate the men?

Did he have worldly sorrow and just quit?

Did he make other bad decisions?

No!
He turned back to God and sought him with his all.
Where are you right now?

It doesn't matter. The grace of God is more than enough to meet your need. All you need to do is go to him.

You can recover all!

David: God the True Reality

David had not had a relationship with God for 16 months. He was leading his men and all their families to the side of the enemy.

The Lord intervened and got David out of the battle, but there were consequences.

Now:

David wept, until he couldn't weep, was on the verge of being stoned by his men.

**But David found strength in the Lord his God.
(1 Samuel 30:6, NIV)**

What does it take for us?

When do we realize we have had enough of sin, impurity, pride, selfish ambition, lukewarmness, bitterness, attitudes, addictions that we turn back to God with all our hearts?

When David turned back to God:

This is a great example of godly sorrow. He realized all that he had done the past sixteen months. He clearly saw all of his bad decisions. He acknowledged his compromise with sin, the corruption he more than welcomed, and finally, the impending destruction this action sought. He felt the pain of all the men who entrusted him with everything they had. He was their leader. He was their shepherd. He led them all astray.

If you are a leader in any area of life, how do you respond to failure caused by your lack of leadership?

Do you act as though you were unaware of the circumstances?

Do you blame others?

Do you play the victim?

Are you prone to using manipulation?

How do you respond?

We have seen the response of Saul.
How should a true godly leader respond?

David wept with them and wept for them. He, in an instant, came to his senses.
The first sin, which led to all else, was not inquiring of the Lord. Isn't it the same with us?

We are so overwhelmed with the Saul's in our lives. We lose heart and, after a while, begin to doubt that God will ever deliver us from the enemy or situation.
How does an elder or minister of the Lord fall into adultery? How does a spiritual businessman give in to cheating and doctoring the books?

It all starts with relying on our own strength and wisdom.

David's son would later declare:

Trust in the Lord with all your heart;
do not depend on your own understanding.
Seek his will in all you do,
and he will show you which path to take.
(Proverbs 3:5–6, NLT)

The truth is that victory comes once we turn to the Lord. Godly sorrow leads to repentance and salvation. This is what David did.

A millennium later the Apostle Paul would declare:

For godly grief produces a repentance not to be
regretted and leading to salvation, but worldly
grief produces death. (2 Corinthians 7:10,
HCSB)

What was the response of our Lord?

This is the best part of all. The Lord always has a plan. He is never surprised, confused or out of control. It is his will that will be done.

Here we are able to examine the heart of Hashem.

Did he respond like us?

David, you need to get retrained before you can be used by me again.
Lack of true forgiveness!
David, you need to be on probation for 16 months to prove your repentance.
Lack of faith to allow grace and mercy!
David, it will take a while before you win back my trust!
Lack of heart to truly let free from offense!
No!

> *"Pursue them," he answered. "You will certainly overtake them and succeed in the rescue." (1 Samuel 30:8, NIV)*

God forgave him on the spot.
Later, David recovered all!
We can also!

A question to consider about the Lord during David's spiritual departure:

What was God doing while David was living in sin?

He is never dull. He never sleeps.

> **He will not let you be defeated.**
> **He who guards you never sleeps.**
> **He who guards Israel**
> **never rests or sleeps.**
> **The Lord guards you.**
> **The Lord is the shade that protects you from the**
> **sun. (Psalm 121:3–5, NCV)**

What was the Almighty doing?

Please feel the power and majesty of the will and also the true grace given by the Most High.

> **These were the men who came to David at**
> **Ziklag, while he was banished from the presence of Saul son of Kish (they were among the**
> **warriors who helped him in battle; 2 they were**
> **armed with bows and were able to shoot arrows**
> **or to sling stones right-handed or left-handed;**
> **they were kinsmen of Saul from the tribe of**
> **Benjamin) (1 Chronicles 12:1–2 MSG)**

While God was not even a thought in David's mind, God was preparing him to be king once he found strength in the Lord his God!

> **They helped David against raiding bands, for all of them were brave warriors, and they were commanders in his army. 22 Day after day men came to help David, until he had a great army, like the army of God. (1 Chronicles 12:21–22 NLT)**

While we would consider David a fall away, tanking it, living as an unbeliever, God put together a great army like the army of God!

If you add all these men, including once David was king in Hebron it is about 350,000 men.

Wow!

God is the true reality.

His grace is sufficient even in our pitiful weakness!

Where are you right now?

To conclude this chapter:

While we are distracted and consumed by the things of this world, think about what the Lord is planning and working on behind the scenes?

Who knows what is awaiting you once you turn back to, or for the first time, truly turn to God?

The question is: when will you come to your senses and turn back to Hashem?

Trust me he is earnestly waiting.

He is more than willing, are you?

Chapter 10 Questions to Ponder

1. What inspired you about this chapter? Why?

2. How do you view God's grace in your life?

3. Do you believe that God has an incredible plan for your life? What? Please explain.

4. If not, what will need to happen for you to seek the Lord with all of your heart?

5. Do you have faith that you can recover all? Are you ready?

6. What do you think Jehovah is doing behind the scenes in your life?

MICHAEL P. WATERMAN

Answers to end of chapter questions

Chapter 11

The Shepherd Is Made King

As we move forward in David's life and journey with the Father, let's view his noteworthy coronation. We have been building up to this point. It had been a long time coming. We saw in the last two chapters that he was on the threshold of this, but let his frustration with Saul make him turn away from the Lord. He is now getting to the point of proverbially punching the ball in for the touchdown. It has been a long and painful journey.

Let's review his walk to the throne.

As a teenage shepherd of the sheep, young David was called, chosen and anointed king by the prophet Samuel.

> *Samuel poured the oil on David's head while his brothers watched. At that moment, the Spirit of the Lord took control of David and stayed with him from then on. (1 Samuel 16:13, CEV)*

This began his decade-plus adventure to become king. He served Saul as a harp player, relieved his torment, defeated Goliath, became a hero to the people, and then had it all taken away. He learned the art of solitude and dependence on Jehovah. He lived in a cave, roamed the desert, and trained disgraced men to be the army of the Lord. He endured the threat that was Saul. He passionately thrived while being a man who was running for his life. He turned to the side of the enemy. He lost his faith and suffered the consequences. He lost it all, and then found strength in God.

It has been an incredible journey. And now the promise of the Lord is manifested in the life of this quite relatable man.

We jump ahead. David is made king.

King David

Later, David prayed to the Lord, saying, "Should I go up to any of the cities of Judah?" The Lord said to David, "Go." David asked, "Where should I go?" The Lord answered, "To Hebron." (2 Samuel 2:1–4a, NCV)

As is now his custom, David seeks the Lord's guidance. He has endured with the King of kings leading his path.

So David went up to Hebron with his two wives: Ahinoam from Jezreel and Abigail, the widow of Nabal from Carmel. David also brought his men and their families, and they all made their homes in the cities of Hebron. Then the men of Judah came to Hebron and appointed David king over Judah. (2 Samuel 2:2-4, NCV)

The day arrived. David was made king. He was the king of Judah. The choice of the Lord was raised from the sheep pen to the kingship.

We see David was led by the Lord. He inquired and received direction from the Most High. He continued waiting and trusting in Hashem. He was given the Southern Kingdom. This was the smaller of the two kingdoms. He continued to allow the Lord to prepare him to be able to lead the people of God as a united and unified kingdom.

If we look at the contrast of good and evil, the separation grows as time passes. In our lives, certain decisions seem to be for us a fork in the road. At first, the distance is not that long. Over time, it seems like two totally different paths. For David, his life contrasted the direction of Saul and later the house of Saul. Good grows more and more powerful while evil becomes more and more pathetic.

> *The war between the house of Saul and the house of David dragged on and on. The longer it went on the stronger David became, with the house of Saul getting weaker. (2 Samuel 3:1, MSG)*

David let the Lord do his work and raise him up. He did not use his own effort to rise to power. He became a man focused on being a vessel to be used and guided by the Heavenly One.

David let the Lord direct his steps. As we looked at last chapter, his son Solomon would write:

> *Trust in the Lord with all your heart,*
> *and do not rely on your own understanding;*
> *think about Him in all your ways,*
> *and He will guide you on the right paths.*
> *(Proverbs 3:5–6, HCSB)*

We continue in our study.

> *Before long all the tribes of Israel approached David in Hebron and said, "Look at us—your own flesh and blood! In time past when Saul was our king, you were the one who really ran the country. Even then GOD said to you, 'You will shepherd my people Israel and you'll be the prince.'" (2 Samuel 5:1–5, MSG)*

The time arrived for the people to follow the plan of God. They understood their chosen leader's calling.

> *All the leaders of Israel met with King David at*
> *Hebron, and the king made a treaty with them*
> *in the presence of GOD. And so they anointed*
> *David king over Israel. (2 Samuel 5:3, MSG)*

At the age of thirty-seven and a half, David became the leader of all Israel. He was thirty when appointed king of Judah, and now the king of all the people of Jacob.

> *David was thirty years old when he became*
> *king, and ruled for forty years. In Hebron*
> *he ruled Judah for seven and a half years. In*
> *Jerusalem he ruled all Israel and Judah for*
> *thirty-three years. (2 Samuel 5:4-5, MSG)*

David defeated all the enemies of Israel. The land was now Israel's. He became the promised shepherd of Israel.

The Blessing Arrives

The promise to Abraham was now fulfilled.

> *GOD told Abram: "Leave your country, your*
> *family, and your father's home for a land that I*
> *will show you. (Genesis 12:1–3, MSG)*

This is where it all began for the people of Hashem.

> *I'll make you a great nation*
> *and bless you.*
> *I'll make you famous;*
> *you'll be a blessing.*
> *I'll bless those who bless you;*
> *those who curse you I'll curse.*
> *All the families of the Earth*

will be blessed through you." (Genesis 12:2-3, MSG)

This referred to the people, nation and soon to come blessing. It had been some time since the promise was made to Abraham. It was being manifested in the life and rule of King David.

David recovered all and defeated all. The Lord was with him, and created a humble heart in him, to follow and lead the people.

Now take a few minutes to really think about David's life. Please consider the challenges and trials he endured. Remember his suffering of loss, betrayal, and the pain he so often endured. He was directly trained by God to lead the flock of Hashem. After nearly twenty years since being anointed by Samuel, David was the king of all Israel.

How does your life look right now?

Are you going through trials, affliction, sorrow, loss, or pain?

Do you see your time of blessing coming?

Does it seem a million miles away?

It might just be coming soon. Your loss and pain will soon lead to blessing and joy. Please allow the Lord to build a place of faith and hope in your heart. Let him give you what is needed to take you from your sheep pen to the incredible plans he has planned just for you. Remember the Lord always has a plan.

We have been studying the life of a godly man. He had his ups, his downs, and all else. He went from the unnoticed shepherd of the small group of sheep to the king, and shepherd, of all Israel.

From a personal perspective, this book and the following written works are the manifestation of the promise of God in my life. It had been a deeply painful, lonely, and sorrow-filled past half dozen years plus for my wife and me. I have had times of despair, extreme loneliness, and overwhelming sorrow. I have felt rejection and times where I felt like the Most High had forgotten me. Yet all the sadness, loneliness, and sorrow, led to what you have before you. I am of the belief, and even more, the conviction, that the more we endure and suffer, the sweeter the blessing. The key to the life of David, and for that matter, those we consider heroes in the faith, is that they did not let the promises, blessings, and revelations be their focus or their reward. Like Abraham, they:

> *After this, the word of the Lord came to Abram*
> *in a vision:*
>
> *"Do not be afraid, Abram.*
> *I am your shield,*
> *your very great reward." (Genesis 15:1, NIV)*

The key is to instead focus on the One who gives blessings, the One who promises, and the One who gives revelations.

Solomon would author:

> *Hope deferred makes the heart sick,*
> *but a dream fulfilled is a tree of life. (Proverbs*
> *13:12, NLT)*

If the young shepherd could go all the way to become king despite his challenges, failures, and pitfalls, what is the coronation God is planning for you?

Chapter 11 Questions to Ponder

1. Are you going through a period of trials and pain? Please explain.

2. Do you focus on the suffering now or the future blessing?

3. What have you learnt from the life of David so far?

4. Are you in the custom of inquiring of the Lord?

5. Do you trust in your own wisdom or are you God reliant?

Answers to end of chapter questions

Chapter 12

Obedience Is Key

As we have looked in the life of David, we have seen that he was a man who desired to please God. He wanted all the glory and praise to go to Hashem. He wrote numerous Psalms in honor of Jehovah. In his life, more often than not, he was obedient to the Will of God. As we have seen, and will examine later, when he did not obey God, the results were devastating.

Our lives are similar. Please take a moment to examine the state of your life when you are obedient to the scriptures and when you are disobedient to the call of the Almighty. There is a drastic difference.

A great song by the group 4him is called Psalm 112. "Blessed is he who fears the Lord who finds delight in his commands" is the chorus. It is amazing how much simpler and less chaotic life becomes when we fear God and just obey his decrees.

How much needless pain is avoided when we simply do one thing: obey?

From the words of the Messiah:

> *Those who know my commands and obey them are the ones who love me, and my Father will love those who love me. I will love them and will show myself to them."*
> *Jesus answered, "If people love me, they will obey my teaching. My Father will love*

*them, and we will come to them and make our
home with them. Those who do not love me do
not obey my teaching. This teaching that you
hear is not really mine; it is from my Father,
who sent me. (John 14:21, 23–24, NCV)*

How are you doing in your spiritual walk when it comes to obedience?

It will tell a lot about where you are, and what is transpiring in your life. We all blow it and disobey the Lord more than we would like to admit.

In this chapter, we will see the blessings of obedience and the consequences of disobedience in King David's life.

The Heart of Obedience

The psalmist declared:

*Shout praises to the Lord!
The Lord blesses everyone
who worships him and gladly
obeys his teachings. (Psalm 112:1, CEV)*

The scriptures are clear. Obedience is essential to truly walking in the Spirit. The act of obedience is a sign of faith.

Without obedience, there is no true faith!

The longest and most influential psalm is one which discusses the importance of obedience.

*Happy are those who live pure lives,
who follow the Lord's teachings.
Happy are those who keep his rules,
who try to obey him with their whole heart.
They don't do what is wrong;
they follow his ways.*

LORD, you gave your orders
to be obeyed completely.
I wish I were more loyal
in obeying your demands.
Then I would not be ashamed
when I study your commands.
When I learned that your laws are fair,
I praised you with an honest heart.
I will obey your demands,
so please don't ever leave me. (Psalm 119:1–8,
NCV)

As we closed out the last chapter, we saw the rise of David. After a long time on the run, he was given the Kingdom. The promises of the Lord were granted. He was now, after years of battle, in a time of peace. The surrounding enemies had all been defeated. God had given all to his chosen leader. It is at this point historians say that David opened the territory, from the six thousand miles that Saul had, to over sixty thousand square miles.

He was at a point in his life to bring back the Ark of the Covenant. This was the true physical presence of the Lord. It was stolen during the times of Samuel. The Philistines had been tortured by the presence of God. David had it in his heart to bring the glory of the Lord back to his people.

Again, let's look into Psalm 119.

LORD, teach me your demands,
and I will keep them until the end.
Help me understand, so I can keep your
teachings,
obeying them with all my heart.
Lead me in the path of your commands,
because that makes me happy.
Make me want to keep your rules
instead of wishing for riches.
Keep me from looking at worthless things.

Let me live by your word.
Keep your promise to me, your servant,
so you will be respected.
Take away the shame I fear,
because your laws are good.
How I want to follow your orders.
Give me life because of your goodness. (Psalm
119:33–40, NCV)

The Lord had given all to the man after his own heart. He had granted to David success in all areas. The Most High allowed David to unify all of Israel. This became the heyday for the people of God. After at least a millennium, the promise to Abraham was fulfilled. The calling of the father of the faith declared promises. We looked at this in the last chapter. It was such a significant time in the scriptures.

GOD told Abram: "Leave your country, your
family, and your father's home for a land that
I will show you.

I'll make you a great nation
and bless you.
I'll make you famous;
you'll be a blessing.
I'll bless those who bless you;
those who curse you I'll curse.
All the families of the Earth
will be blessed through you." (Genesis 12:1–3,
MSG)

The promise was a people, the Israelites, a land Israel, and a blessing that would come a millennium later. The blessing was the coming of the Messiah. The Messiah would come from the blood-line of David. After turmoil after turmoil and trials and suffering the people and the land had come to fruition. It was at this point that

King David desired to bring the Ark of the Covenant back where it belonged.

We are going to be examining 2 Samuel 6. In this chapter we will clearly view the importance and necessity of obedience.

Obedience Is Key

> *David again gathered all the chosen men of Israel—thirty thousand of them. Then he and all his people went to Baalah in Judah to bring back the Ark of God. The Ark is called by the Name, the name of the Lord All-Powerful, whose throne is between the gold creatures with wings. (2 Samuel 6, NCV)*

The goal was to bring back the Ark, which was the throne of the Most High.

> *They put the Ark of God on a new cart and brought it out of Abinadab's house on the hill. Uzzah and Ahio, sons of Abinadab, led the new cart which had the Ark of God on it. Ahio was walking in front of it. (2 Samuel 6:3-4, NCV)*

They put the Ark of God on a new cart. This is the essence of this chapter. They used a new cart to move the Ark of God.

> *David and all the Israelites were celebrating in the presence of the Lord. They were playing wooden instruments: lyres, harps, tambourines, rattles, and cymbals. (2 Samuel 6:5, NCV)*

David and all of Israel were celebrating. They were in the presence of the Lord. They were worshipping to the Almighty. They held nothing back. It was a day of glory and praise. All was going great.

Until:

> *When David's men came to the threshing floor
> of Nacon, the oxen stumbled. So Uzzah reached
> out to steady the Ark of God. (2 Samuel 6:6,
> NCV)*

The oxen stumbled, and Uzzah did the common sense thing when moving an object that is not steady. He reached to steady it. This seems normal, right?

All was joyous, until suddenly:

> *The Lord was angry with Uzzah and killed him
> because of what he did. So Uzzah died there
> beside the Ark of God. (2 Samuel 6:7, NCV)*

The Lord became angry. God killed Uzzah!
What happened?

> *David was angry because the Lord had killed
> Uzzah. Now that place is called the Punishment
> of Uzzah. (2 Samuel 6:8, NCV)*

The king became angry at the actions of Hashem. There was great fear and confusion.

> *David was afraid of the Lord that day, and he
> said, "How can the Ark of the Lord come to me
> now?" So David would not move the Ark of the
> Lord to be with him in Jerusalem. Instead, he
> took it to the house of Obed-Edom, a man from
> Gath. (2 Samuel 6:9-10, NCV)*

The day that began with such fervor and praise ended in death and anger. David now feared the Lord, and lost his faith to bring the Ark home. He left the Ark with a man from Gath. Gath is a part of the Philistines, the enemy of the Lord. We looked in an earlier chapter that, while David was in the land of the Philistines, the Lord was preparing an army that included quite a few foreigners. David had won the heart of many a foreigner. This is why the Ark was left where it was.

> *The Ark of the Lord stayed in Obed-Edom's house for three months,*

The Ark remained for three months with the man from Gath. Guess what transpired?

> *and the Lord blessed Obed-Edom and all his family.*
> *The people told David, "The Lord has blessed the family of Obed-Edom and all that belongs to him, because the Ark of God is there."*

Three months had passed, and now it was time for David to bring the Ark of the Lord to his people.

> *So David went and brought it up from Obed-Edom's house to Jerusalem with joy. (2 Samuel 6:11-12, NCV)*

Here we go again. There is joy. This time it was different.

This reminds me of the time I began seeking the Lord. I have a feeling that this story will be repeated in other books. I had a girlfriend, and we were living in sexual immorality. She suggested we go to her church and talk with the pastor. At the same time, I began studying the Bible with a friend who had become a true Christian several years before. So we met with the pastor and asked what is considered sexual immorality and sexual impurity?

I will never forget now, over twenty years later, his response. He said the point of sexual immorality and sexual impurity is intercourse. Even then, I thought, "Wow!"

Then in studying the Bible, it was pointed out to me:

> *But sexual immorality and any impurity or*
> *greed should not even be heard of[a] among you,*
> *as is proper for saints. (Ephesians 5:3, HCSB)*

In another translation, it says that there must not be a hint. You tell me, according to the scriptures, was that pastor right?

How would I have known unless I examined and knew the scriptures for myself?

The road to hell is often times paved with good intentions. Obedience is a salvation issue. David repented.

> *When the men carrying the Ark of the Lord had*
> *walked six steps, David sacrificed a bull and a*
> *fat calf. (2 Samuel 6:13, NCV)*

This time, David examined the Torah and moved the Ark in obedience to God's decrees. He took the time to understand why the results were so disastrous the first time. This time, it was done the Lord's way. There were sacrifices, and the Levites carried the Ark with poles. The Lord was glorified.

> *Then David danced with all his might before*
> *the Lord. He had on a holy linen vest. David*
> *and all the Israelites shouted with joy and blew*
> *the trumpets as they brought the Ark of the*
> *Lord to the city. (2 Samuel 6:14-15, NCV)*

The man seeking the heart of God once again shows why he was chosen to be king of the Lord's people. As in battle, writing the Psalms, and playing the harp, he danced and celebrated the Lord's glory with all his might. He failed the first time, but the second time it was a day no one would forget.

It reminds me of another time I was studying the Bible with a friend. He was a religious man who refused to obey the scriptures when it came to salvation. We looked at conversions in the book of Acts, and he refused to obey. He couldn't humble himself to be obedient to the scriptures, and sadly, he walked away. What a shame to seek the Lord on our own terms rather than yielding to His.

This was a glorious day in the history of Israel, but there are always those who miss the glory of God.

> *As the Ark of the Lord came into the city, Saul's daughter Michal looked out the window. When she saw David jumping and dancing in the presence of the Lord, she hated him. (2 Samuel 6:16, NCV)*

There are always naysayers and negative people in the midst of the people of God. Satan always has a thorn to try to bring us down. It was Michal, the daughter of Saul and David's wife. Remember earlier, she loved him. The word, at this point, said she had hatred in her heart toward the king.

> *David put up a tent for the Ark of the Lord, and then the Israelites put it in its place inside the tent. David offered whole burnt offerings and fellowship offerings before the Lord. When David finished offering the whole burnt offerings and the fellowship offerings, he blessed the people in the name of the Lord All-Powerful. David gave a loaf of bread, a cake of dates, and a cake of raisins to every Israelite, both men and women. Then all the people went home. (2 Samuel 6:17-19, NCV)*

David accomplished his desire to bring back of the Ark of the Covenant. He sacrificed to Hashem, blessed the people, and sent them home with food. What a glorious day. If there was an event to bring a time machine, this was it. The people of God, after an arduous and painful history, finally had their people, land, the chosen king, and the Ark of the Covenant. God did this all through David. If ever there was a time for a family celebration, this was the time. What did he find at home?

> *David went back to bless the people in his home, but Saul's daughter Michal came out to meet him. She said, "With what honor the king of Israel acted today! You took off your clothes in front of the servant girls of your officers like one who takes off his clothes without shame!" (2 Samuel 6:20, NCV)*

She missed the whole point of the matter. She mocked David, and in reality, mocked God. She was not supportive on a day that honored the king, the people, and God.

There is nothing like family to miss the point of our decisions and purpose of our faith.

> *Then David said to Michal, "I did it in the presence of the Lord. The Lord chose me, not your father or anyone from Saul's family. The Lord appointed me to be over Israel. So I will celebrate in the presence of the Lord. (2 Samuel 6:21, NCV)*

He put her in her place. He reminded her that he was the chosen king, and not Saul, her rejected father,. He celebrated the presence of Hashem.

> *Maybe I will lose even more honor, and maybe I will be brought down in my own opinion, but the girls you talk about will honor me!" (2 Samuel 6:22, NCV)*

As a true man of God, he had no problem humbling himself in order to give glory to the Most High.

How does the chapter end?

And Saul's daughter Michal had no children to
the day she died. (2 Samuel 6:23, NCV)

Let's close out this chapter with the point we need to get. David had the right intentions to bring the Ark back to where it belonged. He was praising and worshipping the Lord. He even put the Ark on a new cart. It was an act of honoring God. But the anger of the Lord was provoked.

Why?

In this book, it has been repeated often that obedience is essential. David should have known the commands for moving the Ark. It was clearly described in the Torah written by Moses. He was in error because he didn't know the scriptures.

How about you?

Where in your life are you in error of the scriptures?

The road to hell is paved with good intentions. As I have previously asked, how do you know you are in error of the word of God if you do not know them?

Someone died for doing the common sense thing because of a lack of obedience and knowledge of the word of God. What do you think the consequences will be for your lack of obedience?

The Messiah himself in the last chapter of his sacred word said:

I warn everyone who hears the words of the
prophecy of this book: If anyone adds anything
to these words, God will add to that person the
disasters written about in this book. And if any-
one takes away from the words of this book of
prophecy, God will take away that one's share

*of the tree of life and of the holy city, which are
written about in this book. (Revelation 22:18–
19, NCV)*

The scriptures are clear there are no excuses. Always remember obedience is the key.

Chapter 12 Questions

1. How serious do you take being obedient to the Lord?

2. What moved you in this chapter?

3. Why is obedience so essential in our relationship with the Lord?

4. Are you able to relate with Michal?

5. Why was David a man after the heart of God in this chapter?

Answers to end of chapter questions

Chapter 13

The Temple of the Almighty

We concluded the last chapter seeing the Ark of the Covenant returning to its rightful home with the people of God. David, after missing the mark on the initial attempt to bring back the Ark, took the time to learn God's way for moving it. The people celebrated and worshipped Jehovah. Hashem had given David success in leading the Israelites in victory over all their enemies. There was peace in the land for David.

In this chapter, David, in gratitude from all Jehovah had given him, has it in his heart to build a Temple, a home for the Almighty. He had a heart of thanks. It was for the glory of God, not himself that he wanted to build the Temple. His heart was for honoring and worshipping the Most High. We will be looking at a sermon I have preached on the heart of gratitude. It was David's heart's desire to build the Temple for the Lord.

Before we continue, please consider:

What is your heart's desire for the Lord?

How would you respond if the Lord said no?

This will be the essence of this chapter. David was after God's own heart. He just wanted to please and glorify his Lord.

Is that your heart's desire?

A Heart of Gratitude

We are going to look at a heart that said thanks!
Let's begin with a question to ponder:
What is your biggest dream for God?
What if He says no?
Our text will be from 2 Samuel 7. We will be looking at the heart
of King David.
The main point I want to emphasize is for us to have a heart that
says thanks to the Most High.

> **After the king was settled in his palace and the**
> **Lord had given him rest from all his enemies**
> **around him, he said to Nathan the prophet,**
> **"Here I am, living in a palace of cedar, while**
> **the ark of God remains in a tent." (2 Samuel**
> **7:1–2, NIV)**

At this point in his life he was on the throne, the absolute king of
Israel.
David thought about how much he had been blessed by God.
How often do we think about that? He was living in a castle, had
immense wealth, power, he had it all! It was on his heart to build a
mighty temple for the Lord to dwell.
He had only pleasing and praising God as his motive.
This was his dream for God!

> **Nathan replied to the king, "Whatever you**
> **have in mind, go ahead and do it, for the Lord**
> **is with you." (2 Samuel 7:3, NIV)**

To your dreams for God, Amen! Let's support and pray for the
dreams of one another!
For some, being in the ministry, going on a mission team, serving
in another country, converting parents, siblings, getting married, hav-

ing kids, having faithful kids, dreams of giving generously, and so many more.

Our dreams!

> ***That night the word of the Lord came to Nathan, saying:***
>
> ***"Go and tell my servant David, 'This is what the Lord says: Are you the one to build me a house to dwell in? 6 I have not dwelt in a house from the day I brought the Israelites up out of Egypt to this day. I have been moving from place to place with a tent as my dwelling. 7 Wherever I have moved with all the Israelites, did I ever say to any of their rulers whom I commanded to shepherd my people Israel, "Why have you not built me a house of cedar?" (2 Samuel 7:4–7)***

The Lord does not need us to do anything!
We are to let God lead us, not our own desires!

Take a moment to consider the power and sovereignty of the Lord. There is a song by Steven Curtis Chapman called "Yours." The emphasis of the song is that everything in creation is all His. To believe that God needs anything from us is false. We receive all we have from Him. In this verse, Hashem explains if he wanted anything he would not need to ask.

He tells the prophet Nathan His heart toward David.

> ***"Now then, tell my servant David, 'This is what the Lord Almighty says: I took you from the pasture and from following the flock to be ruler over my people Israel. (2 Samuel 7:8–11)***

We must remember that God is the eternal, Heavenly Father. He desires what is best for us. He only wants us to have faith and obey him. He has a special, unique plan for each of us. He reminds David through Nathan how far he has taken him.

Please consider over the past ten plus years where has the Lord taken you?

As I am writing this, my final draft, it is all by the grace and plan of the Mighty One. It is to his glory. If you were to tell me, even five years ago, that I would be an author of one book, I would not have believed it. As of today, I am almost finished with four. As it has been stated, this will be a five-part book series. It is all by the grace and to the glory of God.

How about you?

David has gone from shepherding a small group of sheep to becoming the king of the people of Jehovah.

Yahweh continued to speak to David:

> *I have been with you wherever you have gone, and I have cut off all your enemies from before you. Now I will make your name great, like the names of the greatest men of the earth. (2 Samuel 7:9, NIV)*

Consider this for your own walk. He is with us wherever we have been. Imagine being told that your name will become great.

> *And I will provide a place for my people Israel and will plant them so that they can have a home of their own and no longer be disturbed. Wicked people will not oppress them anymore, as they did at the beginning. (2 Samuel 7:10, NIV)*

He claims his promise to Abraham in Genesis 12.

> *And have done ever since the time I appointed leaders over my people Israel. I will also give*

you rest from all your enemies. "The Lord declares to you that the Lord himself will establish a house for you: (2 Samuel 7:11, NIV)

He will give David rest from battling with the enemies of the Lord. He will establish a house for David. David wanted to build a house for God, but it is the Lord who will be building a house for David. This is mercy and grace magnified.

God reminds David of where He has taken him from. To think he was a lowly shepherd, not even considered by his family. He was the least of his brothers. Yet God chose him!

From a lowly beginning God made David:

To be the greatest king in the history of Israel the people of the Lord of hosts.

God chose you, He chose me He chose us!

Remember, from Paul:

Brothers, think of what you were when you were called. Not many of you were wise by human standards; not many were influential; not many were of noble birth. But God chose the foolish things of the world to shame the wise; God chose the weak things of the world to shame the strong. He chose the lowly things of this world and the despised things—and the things that are not— to nullify the things that are, so that no one may boast before him. It is because of him that you are in Christ Jesus, who has become for us wisdom from God—that is, our righteousness, holiness and redemption. Therefore, as it is written: "Let him who boasts boast in the Lord." (1 Corinthians 1:26–31, NIV)

How does that make you feel? God chose you!

But:

When your days are over and you rest with your fathers, I will raise up your offspring to succeed you, who will come from your own body, and I will establish his kingdom. He is the one who will build a house for my Name, and I will establish the throne of his kingdom forever. (2 Samuel 7:12–16)

The Will of God was not for David to build the temple, but one of his sons. The throne of the king will be from the blood line of David. The Messiah is a direct descendant from David. The king will be forever from the line of David.

14 I will be his father, and he will be my son. When he does wrong, I will punish him with the rod of men, with floggings inflicted by men. 15 But my love will never be taken away from him, as I took it away from Saul, whom I removed from before you. 16 Your house and your kingdom will endure forever before me [b]; your throne will be established forever.'"

17 Nathan reported to David all the words of this entire revelation.

God said no!

How do you respond when it is your desire to do something for God and he chooses someone else?

How about that position you have been praying for?

How about that special someone to marry?

How about having children?

Whatever you dream about for God?

The answer is no. You are not the person who will be used by God. Someone else gets the position. She marries another man. You are not able to have children. You are not going to be a missionary. The answer is no.

David's dream was not the will of God. It was to be one of his sons.
What is our response when:
The answer from God is no!
For David:
We can read and see:
Later in life, he would supply all the material and direction for the great temple to be built for the honor of God!
His son chosen by God, built it!
What was the response of this man of God for a great heart's desire denied by the Lord?
This is one of the most heartfelt prayers of gratitude in the Bible!
Let's read together:

Oh, how I wish I responded this way when the Lord says no. Let's aim to be able to pray and talk to the Mighty One like this.

A Prayer to Remember

Then King David went in and sat before the Lord, and he said: "Who am I, O Sovereign Lord, and what is my family, that you have brought me this far? (2 Samuel 7:18–29, NIV)

He sat. He talked to the Lord!
As we talk to our close friends or loved ones.
Do we just stop and talk to God?
He sincerely asked God, in a positive humble way;
Why me?
Not in anger or resentment:

Why me?
David prayed this with a heart full of thanks.
From a shepherd of sheep to the greatest
King of Israel!
The victories were all given by God!
He continued:

> **And as if this were not enough in your sight, O
> Sovereign Lord, you have also spoken about the
> future of the house of your servant. Is this your
> usual way of dealing with man, O Sovereign
> Lord? (2 Samuel 7:19, NIV)**

God told him he would always have a descendant on the throne;
And that one of his son's would build the temple!
He is grateful!

> **"What more can David say to you? For you
> know your servant, O Sovereign Lord. (2
> Samuel 7:20, NIV)**

He speaks in the third person, like a child.
He at this point in his life was a man after the heart of God!
He just wanted to say thank you!
I am beginning to truly realize that sometimes the greatest blessings
of God are when he says no! Or not now!
Why was David a man after the heart of God?

> **For the sake of your word and according to your
> will, you have done this great thing and made it
> known to your servant. (2 Samuel 7:21, NIV)**

He praises God for the things He has done for him!
Do we?

212

"How great you are, O Sovereign Lord! There is no one like you, and there is no God but you, as we have heard with our own ears. (2 Samuel 7:22, NIV)

He is praising the mighty Jehovah!
No one is like him, he is great!
He is truly awesome, great, mighty, not us!

And who is like your people Israel—the one nation on earth that God went out to redeem as a people for himself, and to make a name for himself, and to perform great and awesome wonders by driving out nations and their gods from before your people, whom you redeemed from Egypt? (2 Samuel 7:23, NIV)

We are Israel! The people of God!
Think about the wonders he performed in the life of David,
Think about how many miracles he has performed in your life, my life, in our lives!
How does that make you feel?
What is our response?
Thank you, God, for loving me and thank you God for saving my sinful soul!
David is at a point where he could easily be bitter at God.
Lord, I have done so much. I want to do this for you!
God did not give him the reason why at this time.
He could exude pride, selfish ambition!
A resentful heart!
No!

You have established your people Israel as your very own forever, and you, O Lord, have become their God. (2 Samuel 7:24, NIV)

He focuses on the blessings.
This is what I desire to do.
To focus on the will and love of God!
The positive!

> **"And now, Lord God, keep forever the prom-**
> **ise you have made concerning your servant**
> **and his house. Do as you promised" (2 Samuel**
> **7:25, NIV)**

Lord, keep the promises from your word!
Don't take away your presence from me, your spirit, your love, your
salvation!

> **so that your name will be great forever. Then**
> **men will say, 'The Lord Almighty is God over**
> **Israel!' And the house of your servant David will**
> **be established before you. (2 Samuel 7:26, NIV)**

So your name will be great forever!
Rather than responding as we would by focusing on what God has
not done, David:

> **"O Lord Almighty, God of Israel, you have**
> **revealed this to your servant, saying, 'I will**
> **build a house for you.' So your servant has**
> **found courage to offer you this prayer. (2**
> **Samuel 7:27, NIV)**

He offered a prayer!
What a magnificent prayer!

> **O Sovereign Lord, you are God! Your words are**
> **trustworthy, and you have promised these good**
> **things to your servant. (2 Samuel 7:28, NIV)**

We like David are to focus on the promises of God!

Now be pleased to bless the house of your servant, that it may continue forever in your sight; for you, O Sovereign Lord, have spoken, and with your blessing the house of your servant will be blessed forever." (2 Samuel 7:29, NIV)

I know for many of us it has been a difficult period of time.
There have been many dreams and prayers denied or delayed.
We have seen the response of David.
This is the scripture God is calling us to:

Be joyful always; pray continually; give thanks in all circumstances, for this is God's will for you in Christ Jesus. (1 Thessalonians 5:16–18, NIV)

To be joyful!
To pray continually!
To give thanks in all circumstances!
Let's imitate the heart of King David.
He turned what could have been a time of spiritual defeat to a time of victory because he remembered all the Lord had done for him and would continue to do!
He had a heart that simply said, thanks!

In this study of David, we have been looking at the life of a godly man. He began so well. He shepherded and served the sheep with all his heart. He protected them, lead them. He played the harp and sang songs to them. He loved them like he would later love and shepherd the sheep of Israel. He served Saul with the harp. He, by faith, stepped into the battle and defeated the invincible enemy Goliath. He led in the army of Saul. He found the favor of the people. He developed a kinship with Jonathan. He had the respect of the priests and prophets. He did all well.

Over time, the tables turned and he lost all. He lost his faith and made some grievous mistakes. He went from the limelight to a dark and smelly cave. He was all alone. And then the unwanted showed up looking for a leader and a purpose. This ragtag bunch, led by the young shepherd, turned into Israel's greatest army. This whole time, David was on the run from his nemesis, King Saul.

Once again, he turned away from his Lord and lost it all.

At the point of being stoned by his men, David found strength in the Lord.

He recovered all. Saul died in battle as well as Jonathan.

He became king of Hebron, and then king of all Israel. He had lived an exemplary life. He became more and more powerful, and found victory in battle. He brought the Ark back to the people of God. He desired to build a Temple in honor of God. The answer was "no". And in one of the most precious and powerful prayers expresses a heartfelt thanks to Jehovah.

In the next chapter, we are going to examine the one constant sin in his life. This undealt with transgression led to the lowest point of his life. He became more like Saul than himself. We are going to see the fall of a man of God.

To close out this chapter, let's focus on being able to say thanks in any situation we experience in life.

Chapter 13 Questions to Ponder

1. What is your dream for God? Please take the time to elaborate.

2. What if he says no? Please explain.

3. How do your respond when the answer to your prayers is "no"?

4. What hit you when examining the response God expressed to David?

5. What impacted your heart with David's response once he heard the Lord said "no"?

MICHAEL P. WATERMAN

Answers to end of chapter questions

Chapter 14

The Fall of David

We have been looking at the life of a godly man. King David excelled in many areas of his life. We have seen that he had his share of shortcomings as well. There was one glaring weakness in his life. I have purposely overlooked this area, until now.

What is the downfall of many a powerful man?

The biggest temptation was, is, and will forever be, women. In his life, David lived with a great passion in all he did. This was true of his relations with the opposite sex. His morality was the most glaring failure in his life. If we as men are honest, we are all tempted by sexual sin. I know for myself, lust and impurity are a struggle.

Please, as you read the next several chapters, imagine that this is your life being described. Take the time to imagine all your failures in morality, integrity, and most regretful actions written or even better played on a movie screen. It often seems that, when studying the lives of those in scripture, it is not relatable to our present society. I promise, as we examine the fall of this very mortal man, it will hit home.

Think about how easy we can fall into the temptation of sex. In my life, it is amazing how much things have changed during the past twenty-five years. It wasn't that long ago when you had to be creative to find this type of sin. There was no Internet, apps on phones, or hookup sites. Now sin is only a click away. Consider the billions of dollars spent on pornography in this country alone. You can find it at no cost and little thought. How many are falling into adultery as I write and while you read this? Think about how the divorce rate has gone up, the enormous amount of single mothers who have child after child from different men.

How many athletes and celebrities have multiple children from multiple partners? Is it a wonder why each generation has less and less respect for their sexual purity?

If you look back at the past twenty-five years, the amount of sexual content on television, and in even the news, is mind blowing. Don't even get me started about the increase and approval for homosexuality and same-sex marriages. Now transgendered lifestyles are condoned and even applauded. Where has the sexual morality in our society gone?

I promise, this will be looked at in the third book.

For now:

David was a man who loved women. He had way too many wives and way too many children. He had been so successful in other areas and had been a king who did so much right. He had gone to the top. The level of accountability in life decreases as the ladder of life is climbed. He was an unaccountable king because his weakness was overlooked as his power grew. How could one confront this man?

He was a man who had been blessed and raised up by God, but there was a great undealt with weakness.

Let's look:

> *David took on more concubines and wives from Jerusalem after he left Hebron. And more sons and daughters were born to him. These are the names of those born to him in Jerusalem:*
>
> *Shammua,*
> *Shobab,*
> *Nathan,*
> *Solomon,*
> *Ibhar,*
> *Elishua,*
> *Nepheg,*
> *Japhia,*

Elishama,
Eliada,
Eliphelet. (2 Samuel 5:13–16, MSG)

In this chapter, we are going to look at the fall of a godly man. This is a sermon on the fall of David. In previous chapters, we had seen shortcomings and weaknesses in his life. In this chapter, we are going to see the path that his sin took him on. It didn't just happen. Grievous sin is a long process, which begins with compromise and leads to corruption. It finally results in devastation In this chapter, we will see him fail miserably.

In previous failures, the Lord allowed him to recover. Please allow this to be a warning for your life. As I previously explained, don't spend more than you are willing to pay. The devil is always going to bring the bill. We are about to see the bill coming due for David, and he was unable to pay it.

We have looked at the life of king David, the man known for being a man after God's heart!

We have looked at his humble beginning, David and Goliath, the role that Saul and Jonathan played in his life.

The time he spent sixteen months away from God and the grace of the Lord upon him once he repented and was restored.

The friendship of grace between David and Jonathan, the grace David extended to the son of Jonathan.

It has been a wonderful study in the life of a man of God.

At this point in David's life all was well.

There was great victory in trade, battle and spiritual freedom.

But with victory and increased prosperity comes the temptation to stop looking to and at the Lord!

David: The Fall of a Godly Man

In this lesson, we are going to look at the progression of sin in David's life that led to the fall of a godly man!

If we are not careful this could be us!

2 Samuel 11:1–5 (New International Version)

We all know the story of David and Bathsheba.

As we begin consider a question:
What is your biggest regret or failure?
Imagine it written in scripture for all to see.
We all have lapses in judgement.
Remember the opposite of faith is fear.

> **1 In the spring, at the time when kings go off to war, David sent Joab out with the king's men and the whole Israelite army. They destroyed the Ammonites and besieged Rabbah. But David remained in Jerusalem.**

He should have been in the battle!
We look at David and think, what was he doing?

First Sin: Laziness!

Wait a minute!
Where are we?
Where are our lives?

Where is our focus?
How often are we in the word of God?
How deep is our prayer life?
How open with our struggles are we?
Who are we studying with and helping become right with God?
What happened to David?
He was relaxing, taking a vacation.
He was away from the battle!
He couldn't sleep. He was not tired he was bored.
He lost sight of his mission.
Can anyone relate?

I don't know about you, but it is times of peace that I am most tempted. The thought to think and then look and then sin is there. Satan attacks us at our weakest point.

Where is your point of weakness?

> *2 One evening David got up from his bed and walked around on the roof of the palace. From the roof he saw a woman bathing. The woman was very beautiful,*

Second Sin: Lust!

He had noticed this very beautiful woman.
Sin then built itself up.

The power of the look that turns to lust is intoxicating. Some allow lust to be their addiction. It is not the first look that devastates. The same way that it is not the first drink. It is the increasing desire for more. Addictions are never satisfied. The appetite grows and grows and grows.

James describes the road from compromise to corruption to devastation.

> *When tempted, no one should say, "God is tempting me." For God cannot be tempted by evil, nor does he tempt anyone; but each one is tempted when, by his own evil desire, he is dragged away and enticed. Then, after desire has conceived, it gives birth to sin; and sin, when it is full-grown, gives birth to death. (James 1:13–15, NIV)*

We looked at this before.

Sin is sin!
It builds itself up!

and David sent someone to find out about
her. The man said, "Isn't this Bathsheba, the
daughter of Eliam and the wife of Uriah the
Hittite?" (2 Samuel 11)

Back in this time, the naming of a father, maybe a grandfather
would be mentioned, with respect to someone.
The husband's name would not be mentioned!

He was trying to get the attention of the unaccountable king.
The attendant was a man. He had seen this woman. The sacred word
describes her as very beautiful. The word does not flatter. She was a
thing to admire or desire. This is not a clueless warning. He knew
how the king operated with women.

"Isn't this Bathsheba, the daughter of Eliam
and the wife of Uriah the Hittite?" (2 Samuel
11:3, NIV)

Third Sin: Pride

Whoever loves discipline loves knowledge,
but he who hates correction is stupid. (Proverbs
12:1, NIV)

How open are we to the input of others?

If I think about the mistakes I have made, and continue to
make, it is often a result of pride and not listening to advice. I think
that I know better.

The mistake could have ended right there, but with pride comes
greater consequences.

I know so many who refuse correction or advice because they
think they know better. They rush into bad decisions and suffer the
consequences.

The verse describes this as stupid.

How does David respond?

> **Then David sent messengers to get her. She**
> **came to him, and he slept with her. (She had**
> **purified herself from her uncleanness.) Then**
> **she went back home. (2 Samuel 11:4, NIV)**

Fourth Sin: Adultery!

It just happened, right?
No!
What is our biggest sin?
Our deep-down temptation:
The heart of lust, pornography, addictions, greed, criticalness, lazi-
ness, bitterness lack of openness, or forgiveness!
It will catch up to us!
David was a man of passion!
In all he did. Passion!
He had so many wives, concubines, and so many children.
He obeyed the Lord in all things.
But one!
He continually added wives and concubines against the word of
God!
He, like us refused to deal with the true sin of his heart!
He thought he was stronger than he really was!
When someone leaves the Lord; it is not a one-step action.
The action of divorce, adultery, addiction, immorality, greed, and
bitterness it just doesn't happen!
It is conceived and continues with undealt with sin.
It grows and inevitably it kills us.
What is the lesson here?

Paul declared:

> **These are all warning markers—danger!—in**
> **our history books, written down so that we**

don't repeat their mistakes. Our positions in the story are parallel—they at the beginning, we at the end—and we are just as capable of messing it up as they were. Don't be so naive and self-confident. You're not exempt. You could fall flat on your face as easily as any-one else. Forget about self-confidence; it's use-less. Cultivate God-confidence. (1 Corinthians 10:12, The Message)

This verse of scripture calls us to be warned. Let's be careful to not repeat the mistakes of those before us. In the same way, let us not fail as those often do in our own time.

How often when struggling with sin it is our response to say I am fine?

I don't need help!
David in this time in his life forgot the Lord, our God!
Have we?

The woman conceived and sent word to David, saying, "I am pregnant." (2 Samuel 11:5)

It caught up to him!
The sin of David affected so many lives for a long time!

How often we hear of an adulterous affair result in "oops, I'm pregnant"?

How many one-night hookups result in the same?

Whatever our sin is, if undealt with, it will bring us down. And remember, the truth will come out.

If you add it up; David was not in the battle, had given into laziness, and looked where he shouldn't: lust. He inquired of the lust, pride, continued his pursuit, and it all added up to adultery. And a little while later, she was pregnant.

It will catch up to us as well!
It will affect our future and those close to us as well!

David's Response

How did this godly man respond?

We are about to witness the complete failure of David. His morality, integrity, and heart were all way off. The truth is that it can easily happen to any of us. No one is above moral failure.

We are going to see what we would expect from Saul, not David. Please remember he was, after all, just a man.

We all fall so short!

> **So David sent this word to Joab: "Send me Uriah the Hittite." And Joab sent him to David. (2 Samuel 11:6–17, NIV)**

David had sent for Uriah the Hittite, the husband of Bathsheba.

David, the man after the heart of God, called him to confess his sin, apologize and make things right, right?

Wrong!

Prepare yourself to see a trick out of the play book of Saul.

> **When Uriah came to him, David asked him how Joab was, how the soldiers were and how the war was going. Then David said to Uriah, "Go down to your house and wash your feet." So Uriah left the palace, and a gift from the king was sent after him. But Uriah slept at the entrance to the palace with all his master's servants and did not go down to his house.**

When David was told, "Uriah did not go home," he asked him, "Haven't you just come from a distance? Why didn't you go home?"
Uriah said to David, "The ark and Israel and Judah are staying in tents, and my master Joab and my Lord's men are camped in the open fields. How could I go to my house to eat and drink and lie with my wife? As surely as you live, I will not do such a thing!"
Then David said to him, "Stay here one more day, and tomorrow I will send you back." So Uriah remained in Jerusalem that day and the next. At David's invitation, he ate and drank with him, and David made him drunk. But in the evening Uriah went out to sleep on his mat among his master's servants; he did not go home. (2 Samuel 11:7-13, NIV)

David was hoping to hide his sin!
He tried to in effect manipulate the situation so Uriah would sleep with his wife.
If that happened, the baby was the husband's and problem solved!

This is so unlike David. He was living a lie. I have found that, when a man lives in adultery, he becomes very dumb.

David did all he could to manipulate the situation. He did all he could to make Uriah sleep with his wife, so David could be off the hook. He continued to build his own destruction.

No matter how hard he tried to manipulate Uriah, it did not work.

He should have been convicted with seeing a heart like his own but unconfessed sin leads to more sin.

Uriah was a righteous man. He refused to take advantage of the situation.

He was one of David's fighting men.
This should have broken David, the integrity and loyalty of Uriah
but he had lost sight of God!

Fifth Sin: Deceit!

**In the morning David wrote a letter to Joab
and sent it with Uriah. 15 In it he wrote, "Put
Uriah in the front line where the fighting is
fiercest. Then withdraw from him so he will be
struck down and die."**

**So while Joab had the city under siege, he
put Uriah at a place where he knew the stron-
gest defenders were. When the men of the city
came out and fought against Joab, some of the
men in David's army fell; moreover, Uriah the
Hittite died. (2 Samuel 11:14-17, NIV)**

As Saul once attempted to do to him, David tried to allow the
enemy to kill this man of integrity. David put the man's murder note
in his own hand. The victim, in this sin, was giving the order for
his own death to his leader in battle. Joab was not a stupid man. He
quickly put two and two together.

Old Joab, what a character he was. Let's just say he was David's
henchman.

In earlier times, he and his brothers got David into some hot
water.

In a later book about David, I will dig into this man Joab's life.

For now, he was leading the army while David was relaxing. He
knew David's propensity to have women, and he knew the beauty of
this particular wife. He gladly initiated the death of Uriah.

How sad. For Saul, David survived all his tricks. For David, the
same plan that failed for Saul, worked for him.

This was not necessary.

Sixth Sin: Murder!

He planned the death of Uriah!
Why?
In a ridiculous strategic plan, he set in place the murder of a righteous man so his sin could be hidden!

So let's add up once again. David tries to cover his own behind by getting Uriah drunk and manipulating him to lie with his already pregnant wife. It does not work.

How did this man after the heart of God respond?

He ordered the death of an innocent man.

He lost sight of God!

> **When Uriah's wife heard that her husband was dead, she mourned for him. (2 Samuel 11:26–27, NIV)**

The death of Uriah was found out by Bathsheba.

I wonder what she thought about all this. Her grandfather was a trusted advisor to David. She knew the story of the king. She probably enjoyed the pursuit of David. She was most likely flattered. She was bathing naked in the king's view. She knew that he would be able to see her. It was an affair. It was mutually enjoyable, I suppose. I wonder how she felt hearing about David's deceit and manipulation.

She was pregnant with the king's child. She hears that her husband is killed in battle.

The result:

> **After the time of mourning was over, David had her brought to his house, and she became his wife and bore him a son. (2 Samuel 11:27, NIV)**

David married her. The baby was born.
It was a son!

So after all this they are married.
What do the people think?
Again, this was simple math, people are not dumb.
Why would the king marry a married woman who is pregnant?
The simple answer, he was the father.
Adulterous men are dumb!
Through all this, there is one whom David did not consider.
He forgot about the God who raised him from the sheep pen to the kingdom.

Seventh Sin: Living in the Dark!

David was free and in the clear, right?
He had a great time living in sin and away from God, right?

It worked right? Uriah was killed and David married the woman.
The baby was born. It worked?
No!

> **But the thing David had done displeased the**
> **Lord. (2 Samuel 11:27, NIV)**

The thing that David did displeased the Lord!
Next time, we will look into the results of David's sin more intently.
For now:
How was David living during this time?

> **When I refused to confess my sin,**
> **my body wasted away,**
> **and I groaned all day long.**
> **Day and night your hand of discipline was**
> **heavy on me.**

*My strength evaporated like water in the sum-
mer heat. (Psalm 32:3–4, NLT)*

*David lived in misery for over a year!
To close out: notice the progression of sin:*

David: The Fall of a Godly Man

*David was at a point in his life where he was completely
unaccountable.
He lost his passion for the Lord!
He had a progression of sin:*

1. **Laziness**
2. **Lust**
3. **Pride, not listening to a warning**
4. **Adultery**

He committed adultery. She became pregnant!

David's Response

David responded to his sin by committing more sin!

5. **Deceit**
6. **Murder**
7. **Living in the dark**

The result of the fall of this godly man:

**But the thing David had done displeased the
Lord.**

*Where are we?
This is not the end of the story.*

Next time we will see the grace of God and also the consequences of sin!

Remember God was there throughout it all.

Even through all this David was still a man after God's heart!

Let's remember the love and grace of God!

> **He remembered us in our weakness.**
> **His faithful love endures forever.**
> **He saved us from our enemies.**
> **His faithful love endures forever.**
> **He gives food to every living thing.**
> **His faithful love endures forever.**
> **Give thanks to the God of heaven.**
> **His faithful love endures forever. (Psalm 136:23–26, NLT)**

When looking at the life of David as well as that of ours there is one constant:

The grace of God!

Please, before going to the next chapter, seriously examine the end-of-the-chapter questions. I implore that if you are thinking about, began, are in the middle of, or presently involved in this type of sin, find someone you trust and get it out. There is always the opportunity to turn back to God. Please don't wait until the consequences are more than you are able to handle. Don't wait until the bill coming due is far more than you are able to repay.

Chapter 14 Questions to Ponder

1. What is your biggest struggle when it comes to sin?

2. Do you allow yourself to be accountable?

3. Have you had a progression of sin that led you to regret?

4. Do you struggle with deceit and manipulation?

5. What will you change in respect to your accountability as a result of this chapter?

Answers to end of chapter questions

Chapter 15

The Grace of God

In the last chapter, we saw the fall of David. It was a long time coming. He had that character defect that was never confronted. It built and built until the day of reckoning came. David had an adulterous affair, deceived his way to murder, and lived life without the true source of his strength, the Lord.

If we are honest, we all fall short in our integrity, morality, and self-control. We are, more than likely, guilty of these failures more often than we would like to admit. If we are even more frank, we realize that some of our struggles are character defects. We seem to always be fighting these issues. We are more tempted than others to fail in certain circumstances. The key is, so is everybody else. Remember, we are human.

This is where the grace of God comes in. Who is without character weaknesses, shortcomings, and just plain old sin?

We are all in need of the grace of God. It is a resource we all can go to. The question is, do we go to the Most High with our failures?

We are studying the life of a man who, in most areas of his life, was exemplary. He had his share of failure, pain, and affliction. Who doesn't?

The difference is that his sin and his moral and ethical failures are in print for all to examine. Please take a moment and consider how your life would look if it were being examined with detailed references to your sin and failures. It is all laid out there to be viewed.

Imagine, for a moment, if the battles we have had with immorality, impurity, addiction, adultery, and all else were readable to all. Please keep this focus. Imagine if our pride and arrogance were written for all to see? How do you think we would wish to be viewed?

David was a man just like us. He had his character flaws and warts just like us. We are studying his life because, in most areas, he is an example of how to be. He truly had a leader's and shepherd's heart. His heart was soft to the things of Hashem.

In his life up to this point, he would always go back to God. This time was different.

At any point, he could have confessed and been on the path to repentance. He did not, and continued to live a lie. It seemed that no one would confront the king on his moral failures. It seemed like all looked the other way.

> **But the thing David had done displeased the Lord.**

We must remember that nothing is hidden from God. He sees all. When we are alone in the dark it is as clear as day to Hashem. David himself wrote:

> *Where can I go to get away from your Spirit?*
> *Where can I run from you?*
> *If I go up to the heavens, you are there.*
> *If I lie down in the grave, you are there.*
> *If I rise with the sun in the east*
> *and settle in the west beyond the sea,*
> *even there you would guide me.*
> *With your right hand you would hold me.*
>
> *I could say, "The darkness will hide me.*
> *Let the light around me turn into night."*
> *But even the darkness is not dark to you.*

The night is as light as the day;
darkness and light are the same to you. (Psalm
139:7–12, NCV)

Centuries later:

God means what he says. What he says goes.
His powerful Word is sharp as a surgeon's scal-
pel, cutting through everything, whether doubt
or defense, laying us open to listen and obey.
Nothing and no one is impervious to God's
Word. We can't get away from it—no matter
what. (Hebrews 4:12–13, MSG)

We are going to be looking at a follow up sermon from "the fall of David." In this chapter, we will see a few things. We will see the omniscience and omnipresence of the Almighty, the faith of a Prophet, the brokenness, and repentance of David, and throughout it all, we will clearly see the grace of God. This is a convicting message. It is a warning for all of us. If we are living in unconfessed sin, and think we will get away with it, we have another thing coming.

As we have looked at different points in David's life, please consider in your own walk with Yahweh if you are a man like Nathan. Are you willing to obey the Lord and confront sin in a leader even one in your ministry?

In your time in the faith, have you ever been broken like David in this chapter? The last question to consider, are you aware of the power and grace of the Lord in your life?

The Rebuke from a Man of God

Do not be deceived: God cannot be mocked.
A man reaps what he sows. (Galatians 6:7–8,
NIV)

This is the theme scripture for this point in David's life and yours and mine.

God will not be mocked. Do not be deceived.

How do we live?

> **The one who sows to please his sinful nature, from that nature will reap destruction; the one who sows to please the Spirit, from the Spirit will reap eternal life. (Galatians 6:8, NIV)**

In the Old Covenant:

> **"They sow the wind**
> **and reap the whirlwind.**
> **The stalk has no head;**
> **it will produce no flour.**
> **Were it to yield grain,**
> **foreigners would swallow it up. (Hosea 8:7, NIV)**

In other words, we reap what we sow!

Are we in the light or living in darkness?

> **Then the Lord sent Nathan to David. He came to him and said, "There were two men in one city. One was rich and the other was poor. The rich man had many flocks and cattle. But the poor man had nothing except one little female lamb which he bought and fed. It grew up together with him and his children. It would eat his bread and drink from his cup and lie in his arms. It was like a daughter to him. Now a traveler came to the rich man. But the rich man was not willing to take from his own flock or his own cattle, to make food for the traveler who had come to him. Instead, he took the poor**

man's female lamb and made it ready for the man who had come to him." (2 Samuel 12:1–15, NLV)

Then the Lord sent Nathan to David.

God sent Nathan. Remember do not be deceived the Lord will not be mocked!
This prophet is sent as the voice of the Lord.
He tells a story to the King.
David gets angry with the story.

David burned with anger against the man and said to Nathan, "As surely as the Lord lives, the man who did this deserves to die! He must pay for that lamb four times over, because he did such a thing and had no pity." (2 Samuel 12:5-6, NIV)

Isn't it amazing, when we are in unconfessed or unrepentant sin we show little grace toward others.
Then Nathan speaks God's word to David!
Nathan reminds David of the true realm of God!
Four simple three letter words:
You are the man!
Are we?

Nathan said to David, "You are the man!

Finally, after over a year living in shame and guilt, David is confronted.

He is told:

You are the man!

David lost focus of Hashem. He was all alone and powerless. He had lost his strength. He had lost sight of God.

How about us?

Where are we right now?

Are we living in openness to the Lord and others?

If not the consequences can be lethal.

> *This is what the Lord God of Israel says: 'I chose you to be the king of Israel. I saved you from the hand of Saul. I gave you Saul's family and Saul's wives into your care. I gave you the nations of Israel and Judah. And if this were too little, I would give you as much more. (2 Samuel 12:7-8, NIV)*

David was reminded of where he came from.
Do we remember where we come from?

An incredible comment by God for us to consider; if David wanted more, all he had to do was ask. God would have given him more. Think about that!

In our lives, and more specific, our walk with the Lord, the thought that all we need to have is to ask for more and it will be given.

Wow.

Please consider David was the choice of Hashem to be the King of his people.

All is God's. We as his children have an inheritance and a claim to all.

We like David lose focus and fall once we take matters into our own hands.

This could have been avoided. Our biggest failures and sins can be avoided.

But:

> **Why have you hated the Word of the Lord by doing what is bad in His eyes?**

The Lord does not mince words. Hated!
Let's take inventory of why the king hated the King of kings.
Why?

> **You have killed Uriah the Hittite with the sword.**

Murder!

> **You have taken his wife to be your wife.**

Adultery!

> **You have killed him with the sword of the sons of Ammon. (2 Samuel 12:9)**

The result:

> **So now some from your family, even in the future, will die by the sword, because you have turned against Me and have taken the wife of Uriah the Hittite to be your wife.' (2 Samuel 12:10)**

Nothing is hidden from the Lord!
He knows all!
Don't be deceived. The Lord is not going to be mocked!

How about us?
Are we in the word?
Are we living in the light?

Are we open with our sin?
Are we extending forgiveness?
Are we living as true disciples of the Lord?

> **This is what the Lord says: "See, I will bring trouble against you from your own family. I will take your wives in front of your eyes and give them to your neighbor. He will lie with your wives in the light of day. You did it in secret. But I will do this in front of all Israel, and under the sun." (2 Samuel 12:11)**

The consequences of sin!
We will suffer the consequences of our sin!

> **The one who sows to please his sinful nature, from that nature will reap destruction. (Galatians 6:8)**

In studying this man's life, he was never the same after falling into sin with Bathsheba and not turning to the Lord!
We need to be a Nathan to others.
Who are we a Nathan to?
Who do we allow to be a Nathan to us?

At a later time Solomon wrote:

> **5A truly good friend**
> **will openly correct you.**
> **6You can trust a friend**
> **who corrects you,**
> **but kisses from an enemy**
> **are nothing but lies. (Proverbs 27:5–6, CEV)**

Do we have true friends?
Are we a true friend?

God sent Nathan to rebuke David. He openly corrected the king!

He was trustworthy because he cared more about pleasing God than his friend.

Do we?

A friend does not tell us what we want to hear.

A friend tells us what we need to hear!

> **17 As iron sharpens iron,**
> **so a friend sharpens a friend. (Proverbs 27:17**
> **(NLT)**

We all need to hope for a Nathan in our lives and to be a Nathan to other's.

We see in the scriptures that Nathan obeyed the Lord. He was a spiritual man. He cared about pleasing Hashem. He went into the king. He had the respect and trust of David. He told a story to get to the heart of David and to wake him up. David thought no one knew the extent of his sin, but God knew and would not tolerate it any longer.

I believe David was relieved that he was confronted. It is like having to have your knee drained. It will hurt while getting drained, but then there will be relief.

Now is a good time to compare the sins of Saul and David. Some believe the sin of David was far worse than that of Saul. Why was Saul rejected, but David called a man after the heart of God?

The difference between the two was quite simple. When confronted on their sin, Saul took no responsibility while David was broken and repented.

Where do you stand?

What does it mean to repent?

David's Brokenness

After hearing and seeing that his sin was not hidden.
David responds!

> **Then David said to Nathan, "I have sinned**
> **against the Lord." And Nathan said to him,**
> **"The Lord has taken away your sin. You will**
> **not die.**

David was sincere. It was as if all of his sin hit him at once. Some believe it was like a movie playing in his mind, the last year plus of rebellion toward the Lord. He saw and felt his separation from God, and the pain and damage of his sin.

The grace of God is forgiveness and not being put to death.
Incidentally, adultery and murder resulted in death in this time.
Eye for an eye!
The grace we do not deserve!
But the grace of God does not take away the consequences of sin.

> **But by this act you have given those who hate**
> **the Lord a reason to speak against the Lord.**
> **The child that is born to you will die for sure."**
> **Then Nathan went home. (2 Samuel 12:13-14)**

If we sin and break our arm in the process, once we repent, we are forgiven, but we will still have a broken arm.
David spent the rest of his life regretting the day he committed adultery with Bathsheba!
He was forgiven.
But for the rest of his life, he lived in the backwash of his sin.
His children reaped what he sowed!
Loneliness, deceit, incest, rape, rebellion, adultery and murder!
How about us, what will we reap from the way we are living?
How did he respond?

When I kept silent,
my bones wasted away
through my groaning all day long.
For day and night
your hand was heavy upon me;
my strength was sapped
as in the heat of summer. (Psalm 32:3–4, 1–2,
5–8, NIV)

David is describing what it was like for him as he lived in sin and out of fellowship with God!
Some of us are at this point right now!
But at this point after being contrite before the Lord this could be said of David.

Blessed is he
whose transgressions are forgiven,
whose sins are covered.
Blessed is the man
whose sin the Lord does not count against him
and in whose spirit is no deceit. (Psalm 32:1-2,
NIV)

A relationship with God, a forgiven sinner, a disciple of Jesus!
The result:

Then I acknowledged my sin to you
and did not cover up my iniquity.
I said, "I will confess
my transgressions to the Lord—
and you forgave
the guilt of my sin.
Selah

Therefore let everyone who is godly pray to you
while you may be found;

surely when the mighty waters rise,
they will not reach him.

You are my hiding place;
you will protect me from trouble
and surround me with songs of deliverance.
Selah

I will instruct you and teach you in the way you
should go;
I will counsel you and watch over you. (Psalm
32:6-8, NIV)

He repented of his sin!
This is what we need to do!
He confessed his sin.
He went back to praying to his God!
He put his whole trust back into the deliverer!
He instructs us today on how we should live.
In openness, the light!
We must do the same!

This is my favorite Psalm. When I have my times feeling separated from the Most High, due to my sin, it helps to get my heart back on track with Jehovah.

Please feel the prayer of a broken and contrite heart.

Have mercy on me, O God,
according to your unfailing love;
according to your great compassion
blot out my transgressions.
 Wash away all my iniquity
and cleanse me from my sin.
  For I know my transgressions,
and my sin is always before me.
  Against you, you only, have I sinned

and done what is evil in your sight,
so that you are proved right when you speak
and justified when you judge (Psalms 51:1–4,
7–13, 16–17, NIV)

The ultimate response to God's rebuke, open confession!

Cleanse me with hyssop, and I will be clean;
wash me, and I will be whiter than snow.
(Psalm 51:7, NIV)

Purify my heart!

Let me hear joy and gladness;
let the bones you have crushed rejoice. (Psalm
51:8, NIV)

Heal my heart!

Hide your face from my sins
and blot out all my iniquity. (Psalm 51:9, NIV)

Forgive me!

Create in me a pure heart, O God,
and renew a steadfast spirit within me. (Psalm
51:10, NIV)

Strengthen me!

Do not cast me from your presence
or take your Holy Spirit from me. (Psalm
51:11, NIV)

Keep my heart close to you!

Restore to me the joy of your salvation
and grant me a willing spirit, to sustain me.
(Psalm 51:12, NIV)

Lite the fire within my heart again!

Then I will teach transgressors your ways,
and sinners will turn back to you. (Psalm
51:13, NIV)

Allow me to be an example to others of your love!

You do not delight in sacrifice, or I would bring it;
you do not take pleasure in burnt offerings.
The sacrifices of God are [c] **a broken spirit;**
a broken and contrite heart,
O God, you will not despise. (Psalm 51:16-17,
NIV)

The Lord does not care about our actions alone.
We can do and do and do!
He desires our hearts to be broken before him.
We have nothing to give.
We cannot earn his love.
A humble, contrite, broken heart pleases the Lord.

Sacrifices and offerings
are not what please you;
gifts and payment for sin
are not what you demand.
But you made me willing
to listen and obey. (Psalm 40:6, CEV)

Obedience!

My hands made all these things, and so all these things came into being," says the Lord. "But I will look to the one who has no pride and is broken in spirit, and who shakes with fear at My Word. (Isaiah 66:2, NLV)

This led to a change:

Godly sorrow brings repentance that leads to salvation and leaves no regret, but worldly sorrow brings death. (2 Corinthians 7:10, NIV)

David dealt with his sin.
Remember he was a man after God's own heart!
Are we?
How do we deal with our own sin?
Do we repent, or hide and live lives of hypocrites?
What are we sowing?

The sacrifices of God are a broken spirit;
a broken and contrite heart,
O God, you will not despise. (Psalm 51:17)

Remember:

Do not be deceived: God cannot be mocked. A man reaps what he sows. The one who sows to please his sinful nature, from that nature will reap destruction; the one who sows to please the Spirit, from the Spirit will reap eternal life. (Galatians 5:7–8)

Let's be men and women who are after the heart of God!

This chapter is called the grace of God, why?

> *Then David comforted Bathsheba his wife.*
> *He slept with her and had sexual relations*
> *with her. She became pregnant again and had*
> *another son, whom David named Solomon.*
> *The Lord loved Solomon. The Lord sent word*
> *through Nathan the prophet to name the baby*
> *Jedidiah, because the Lord loved the child. (2*
> *Samuel 12:24–25, NCV)*

The Lord allowed the baby born in sin to die, but after the repentance of David another son was born. This baby was loved by the Father. His name was Solomon. The next king of Israel.

To close out this chapter:

We must cling to:

> *We know that in everything God works for the*
> *good of those who love him. They are the people*
> *he called, because that was his plan. (Romans*
> *8:28, NCV)*

Chapter 15 Questions to Ponder

1. Do you have a Nathan in your life?

2. Are you a Nathan to others?

3. Who do you emulate when confronted on your sin Saul or David?

4. How do you respond to Psalm 32, Psalm 40, Psalm 51, and Isaiah 66?

5. Do you see the grace of God in your life? Please explain.

6. What is one thing you will be repenting of after reading this chapter?

Answers to end of chapter questions

Chapter 16

The Sword Shall Not Depart

But the thing David had done displeased the Lord.

What a statement. David was a leader chosen by God. He was held in high honor. He did well in so many areas of his life. He was held to a higher standard by Hashem, as are we who claim to be his followers. How much more leaders in the Kingdom of God?

We examined the progression of his sin. He lived in darkness for over a year. He had ample time to confess and repent. He did not.

We witnessed the rebuke and confrontation of Nathan. We saw the response and contrite brokenness of David. We saw the grace of the Lord.

But:

The title of this chapter is ominous. We all understand that actions are followed by reactions, and eventual consequences. We will see a progression of loss and pain for the king. Imagine this being your life.

Wherever you find yourself as you are reading this, consider the consequences to the actions of this man of God. This can be any of us. We are warned!

The baby died. David was warned that trouble would be knocking and often.

Now therefore, the sword will never leave your
house because you despised Me and took the
wife of Uriah the Hittite to be your own wife.
(2 Samuel 12:10–12, HCSB)

The sword will never leave your house. This meant pain and suffering for the king. He would never forget the sin he committed that displeased his Lord. He would endure intense affliction, loss and regret.

Let these words hit you and think about the sin in your life:

"This is what the Lord says, 'I am going to
bring disaster on you from your own family: I
will take your wives and give them to another
before your very eyes, and he will sleep with
them publicly. You acted in secret, but I will do
this before all Israel and in broad daylight.'" (2
Samuel 12:11-12, NIV)

David lived to see these words more than just come true. After this, he was never the same father or husband.

We are going to look at these words come to fruition in this chapter. We are going to see rape, murder, deceit, and a time where the king was forced to run for his life. These all happened by the hands of David's sons. Pain and suffering were an understatement for the heart of David at this time.

The Fall of the House of David

David had a son named Absalom and a son
named Amnon. Absalom had a beautiful sister
named Tamar, and Amnon loved her. Tamar
was a virgin. Amnon made himself sick just
thinking about her, because he could not find
any chance to be alone with her. (2 Samuel
13:1–22, NCV)

Let's get this straight; David had a son who was in love with his half-sister. Remember, there were so many wives and so many children. They were forced to raise themselves.

Where was David?

He was not involved. He was absent. There is nothing worse in our present generation than the examples of disinterested fathers. Consider the increase of promiscuous woman out there. They are allowing themselves to be treated like prostitutes. They have one affair after the other, and unwanted children are conceived. The increased rate of homosexuality and the disgrace of the transgender community only grow. Why?

This is a result of the lack of men. The lack of godly examples! It is sad to see that, more often than not, a man is more focused on being politically correct than biblically correct. This example of David's failure is more than prevalent in the 'church' culture.

Let's continue:

> **Amnon had a friend named Jonadab son of Shimeah, David's brother. Jonadab was a very clever man. He asked Amnon, "Son of the king, why do you look so sad day after day? Tell me what's wrong!"**
>
> **Amnon told him, "I love Tamar, the sister of my half-brother Absalom." (2 Samuel 13:3-4, NCV)**

I have to ask, where were the children while David worshipped the Lord?

It is so sad how for the most part, wealthy over privileged children grow up imitating the worst from their parents.

The son of David was in love with his half-sister. Think about that. Even here, David was a man who always needed woman around. His son lusted after his own blood.

Who is advising him in this perversion?

Well, a cousin. Family! What did he advise?

> *Jonadab said to Amnon, "Go to bed and act as if you are sick. Then your father will come to see you. Tell him, 'Please let my sister Tamar come in and give me food to eat. Let her make the food in front of me so I can watch and eat it from her hand.'" (2 Samuel 13:5, NCV)*

Lie, deceive, and take advantage of, what great council.

First, trick the king who was oblivious and clueless about what was going on in the lives of his children. The goal was to get him to send his sister to take care of him.

> *So Amnon went to bed and acted sick. When King David came in to see him, Amnon said to him, "Please let my sister Tamar come in. Let her make two of her special cakes for me while I watch. Then I will eat them from her hands." (2 Samuel 13:6, NCV)*

Did it work?

> *David sent for Tamar in the palace, saying, "Go to your brother Amnon's house and make some food for him." (2 Samuel 13:7, NCV)*

Check. It was accomplished.

> *So Tamar went to her brother Amnon's house, and he was in bed. Tamar took some dough and pressed it together with her hands. She made some special cakes while Amnon watched. Then she baked them. (2 Samuel 13:8, NCV)*

The next step was to make it so he was alone with Tamar.

> *Next she took the pan and served him, but he*
> *refused to eat.*
>   *He said to his servants, "All of you, leave*
> *me alone!" So they all left him alone.*

It worked again. Tamar was the daughter of the king. She was sheltered. She had no idea of what she was being set up for. Like her father with Saul, she was very naïve.

Now it was time for the finishing touch.

> *Amnon said to Tamar, "Bring the food into the*
> *bedroom so I may eat from your hand."*
>   *Tamar took the cakes she had made and*
> *brought them to her brother Amnon in the bed-*
> *room. (2 Samuel 13:9-10, NCV)*

He was playing her like an instrument.

How often do we hear about an Uncle or friend of the family molesting an innocent child?

How often are women raped?

Have you ever seen the movie *Spotlight*?

It exposes the molestation of children by priests in a local community. The sad part is it was covered up by many.

To the sadness and tragedy of the innocent victims, it is not an uncommon event.

> *She went to him so he could eat from her hands,*
> *but Amnon grabbed her. He said, "Sister, come*
> *and have sexual relations with me." (2 Samuel*
> *13:11, NCV)*

How did she respond?

> *Tamar said to him, "No, brother! Don't force me! This should never be done in Israel! Don't do this shameful thing! I could never get rid of my shame! And you will be like the shameful fools in Israel! Please talk with the king, and he will let you marry me." (2 Samuel 13:12-13, NCV)*

She had the state of mind to warn him about the consequences of his sin.

> *But Amnon refused to listen to her. He was stronger than she was, so he forced her to have sexual relations with him. (2 Samuel 13:14, NCV)*

He did not listen. He raped his sister.
Then:

> *After that, Amnon hated Tamar. He hated her more than he had loved her before. Amnon said to her, "Get up and leave!" (2 Samuel 13:15, NCV)*

She was a righteous woman. She warned him again.

> *Tamar said to him, "No! Sending me away would be worse than what you've already done!" (2 Samuel 13:16, NCV)*

Did he listen?

> *But he refused to listen to her. He called his young servant back in and said, "Get this*

> *woman out of here and away from me! Lock the*
> *door after her." So his servant led her out of the*
> *room and bolted the door after her. (2 Samuel*
> *13:16-18, NCV)*

He was like a typical spoiled cowardly child who takes what he wants and then just leaves as if nothing happened.

> *Tamar was wearing a special robe with long*
> *sleeves, because the king's virgin daughters*
> *wore this kind of robe. To show how upset she*
> *was, Tamar put ashes on her head and tore her*
> *special robe and put her hand on her head.*
> *Then she went away, crying loudly. (2 Samuel*
> *13:18-19, NCV)*

As is so often the case with this horrific crime; the victim is the one who feels shame and disgrace.

She went to her full brother, they shared the same mother, and what does she find?

> *Absalom, Tamar's brother, said to her, "Has*
> *Amnon, your brother, forced you to have sexual*
> *relations with him? (2 Samuel 13:20, NCV)*

He knew that their half-brother raped his sister, and what does he suggest?

> *For now, sister, be quiet. He is your half-*
> *brother. Don't let this upset you so much!" (2*
> *Samuel 13:20, NCV)*

Here was Absalom, who we will see was a real piece of work. Here we see cowardice and a lack of common decency. She was made to feel as though it was not a big deal. It is sad how true this is today for those who are molested and raped.

The result of this grievous sin:

> *So Tamar lived in her brother Absalom's house*
> *and was sad and lonely. (2 Samuel 13:20,*
> *NCV)*

She lived her life in the carnage of the sins of her father and the wickedness of her brothers. She was never the same. Poor Tamar!

Well David did something right?

> *When King David heard the news, he was very*
> *angry. (2 Samuel 13:21, NCV)*

He was angry and did absolutely nothing. This event should have woken him up and made him more involved with his children. It could have ended here.

But:

> *Absalom did not say a word, good or bad, to*
> *Amnon. But he hated Amnon for disgracing his*
> *sister Tamar. (2 Samuel 13:22, NCV)*

Absalom did not say a word, but he hated his brother for his disgracing his sister. He, as we will see, planned his revenge. He would become the thorn in the side of his father King David.

In another translation:

> *King David heard the whole story and was*
> *enraged, but he didn't discipline Amnon.*
> *David doted on him because he was his first-*
> *born. Absalom quit speaking to Amnon—not a*
> *word, whether good or bad—because he hated*
> *him for violating his sister Tamar. (2 Samuel*
> *13:21–22, MSG)*

Unfortunately, the king, like many modern-day religious leaders, remained clueless about his children. The sword would never depart from the house of David.

It went from bad to worse to the king being forced to flee for his life.

Absalom: From Murder to Revolt

Two years passed. Absalom, the son of David, planned and schemed to extract revenge for his sister Tamar.

> *Two years later Absalom had some men come to Baal Hazor, near Ephraim, to cut the wool from his sheep. Absalom invited all the king's sons to come also. Absalom went to the king and said, "I have men coming to cut the wool. Please come with your officers and join me."*
>
> *King David said to Absalom, "No, my son. We won't all go, because it would be too much trouble for you." Although Absalom begged David, he would not go, but he did give his blessing. (2 Samuel 13:23–27, NCV)*

Here we see the plan of Absalom unfold. He had been planning his revenge for two years. He used a custom in shepherding to trick his oblivious father to hand the head of Amnon to him on a platter.

Let's see manipulation and deceit at work.

> *Absalom said, "If you don't want to come, then please let my brother Amnon come with us." (2 Samuel 13:26, NCV)*

He went out of his way to get his hated brother to come along. He pleaded with David to allow his brother to go.

> *King David asked, "Why should he go with*
> *you?" (2 Samuel 13:26, NCV)*

David seemed to get a clue and connected some dots. He inquired of his son.

> *Absalom kept begging David until he let*
> *Amnon and all the king's sons go with Absalom.*
> *(2 Samuel 13:27, NCV)*

"Just read that," he begged David. If David was truly walking with the Lord, as he had in the past, he would have certainly inquired of God to know his son's true intentions. But David gives in to Absalom, and hands him the smoking gun for Amnon. It was similar to when he tricked Uriah to his death in a previous chapter.

Absalom had his men kill his brother. He planned two years and set up his brother's death to fruition.

We have seen a brother rape his sister and now another brother planning and executing the murder of that brother.

How did David react?

> *David cried for his son every day.*
> *But Absalom ran away to Talmai[a] son of*
> *Ammihud, the king of Geshur. (2 Samuel*
> *13:37, NCV)*

He cried and mourned the loss of his murdered son. Absalom ran away. Once again David did nothing.

Some scholars have hypothesized that David was still dealing with the guilt of his sin with Bathsheba. He was unable to deal with the actions of his children. He had it printed on his mind and in his heart that the sword would never depart from his house.

Absalom was a spoiled child who was never disciplined. He was not confronted for his actions by his father the king. He now planned to take the kingship from his father. This did not have to happen.

When do you deal with the actions of your children?

How far must they drift? How bad must things get?

How about your ministers, bosses?

David could not deal because it would be too painful.

Absalom came back at the request of David after being manipulated by Joab. Good old Joab was another piece of work. He spent two years being ignored by his father. David was unwilling and unable to deal with his son.

Then the time arrived for Absalom to take the kingdom from his father. He planned and manipulated every step of the way.

> *As time went on, Absalom took to riding in a horse-drawn chariot, with fifty men running in front of him. Early each morning he would take up his post beside the road at the city gate. When anyone showed up with a case to bring to the king for a decision, Absalom would call him over and say, "Where do you hail from?"*
>
> *And the answer would come, "Your servant is from one of the tribes of Israel." (2 Samuel 15:1–6, MSG)*

He deceitfully stole the hearts of the people.

> *Then Absalom would say, "Look, you've got a strong case; but the king isn't going to listen to you." Then he'd say, "Why doesn't someone make me a judge for this country?*

He was placing himself above the king. He was bad mouthing his father.

> *Anybody with a case could bring it to me and I'd settle things fair and square." Whenever someone would treat him with special honor,*

he'd shrug it off and treat him like an equal,
making him feel important. Absalom did this
to everyone who came to do business with the
king and stole the hearts of everyone in Israel.
(2 Samuel 15:3-6, MSG)

He was making his way for the throne.
Where was David?

I have always believed that if a spiritual leader is doing the Will of God, there will be no one able to steal his position. The people's needs were not being met. So Absalom played the part of acting concerned and sincere to the people while David was not involved.

As the king, and a father, David failed his son miserably. He never confronted or dealt with the rape of Tamar with his son Amnon. He never allowed Absalom to share how he felt about the rape. He was not in touch to realize that Absalom craved revenge. He was helpless to handle Absalom's murder of Amnon. He was powerless to stop the ambition of his son.

After four years of this, Absalom spoke to the
king, "Let me go to Hebron to pay a vow that I
made to GOD. Your servant made a vow when
I was living in Geshur in Aram saying, 'If GOD
will bring me back to Jerusalem, I'll serve him
with my life.'" (2 Samuel 15:7-8, MSG)

Four years had passed and Absalom really played his father. He had no desire to please or devote his life to Hashem. It was a complete mockery.

Did David inquire of the Lord at all during this time?

He does not. As we see in his response.

The king said, "Go with my blessing." And he got
up and set off for Hebron. (2 Samuel 15:9, MSG)

He continued to condone his children's bad behavior.

Absalom was planning his revolution. David was then hit with a rude awakening.

> *Someone came to David with the report, "The whole country has taken up with Absalom!" (2 Samuel 15:13, MSG)*

What? The sword will not depart from your family.

> *"Up and out of here!" called David to all his servants who were with him in Jerusalem. "We've got to run for our lives or none of us will escape Absalom! Hurry, he's about to pull the city down around our ears and slaughter us all!" (2 Samuel 15:14, MSG)*

The king was once again forced to flee and be on the run for his life.

He and those loyal to him were forced to flee the city of David. He was betrayed on many fronts. He was insulted on his way to hiding. It all seemed lost.

The bill for our sins will always come due. As described in earlier chapters, cowardly, rebellious leaders produce similar fruit. David was reaping what he had sown in his children. It did not need to happen.

This leads to a time where David was at war with his son for the kingdom. Time passed and the wise crafty king uses his experience in battle to outsmart and overthrow his son. David had men on the inside still loyal to him and knew his son's plans in advance. In a sense, he gave Absalom the rope and his son hung himself.

As with all military battles, there are always casualties. David ordered his men to bring his son to him alive. He still felt there could be reconciliation.

> *The king commanded Joab, Abishai, and Ittai, "Be gentle with young Absalom for my sake."*

Everyone heard the king's orders to the commanders about Absalom. (2 Samuel 18:5:9–17, NCV)

The battle played out. It was a fight to see who would be the king. Isn't it interesting? David was the chosen king, Saul was the rejected king, and young Absalom was the self-appointed king. As the case is in the life of David, the Lord of hosts gave the victory to his choice for king.

Then Absalom happened to meet David's troops. As Absalom was riding his mule, it went under the thick branches of a large oak tree. Absalom's head got caught in the tree, and his mule ran out from under him. So Absalom was left hanging above the ground. (2 Samuel 18:9, NCV)

What an ironic result. His big head was caught and led to his defeat. I guess his head was just too big.

When one of the men saw it happen, he told Joab, "I saw Absalom hanging in an oak tree!"
Joab said to him, "You saw him? Why didn't you kill him and let him fall to the ground? I would have given you a belt and four ounces of silver!" (2 Samuel 18:10-11, NCV)

Joab was the leader of David's army. He did not obey the king. He had revenge on his own mind.

The man answered, "I wouldn't touch the king's son even if you gave me twenty-five pounds of silver. We heard the king command you, Abishai, and Ittai, 'Be careful not to hurt young Absalom.' If I had killed him, the king

would have found out, and you would not have
protected me!" (2 Samuel 18:12-13, NCV)

His soldier obeyed the king. So Joab took matters into his own hands. Against a direct order of David, he disobeyed and killed his king's son.

Joab was, as you see, a piece of work.

> *Joab said, "I won't waste time here with you!"*
> *Absalom was still alive in the oak tree, so Joab*
> *took three spears and stabbed him in the heart.*
> *Ten young men who carried Joab's armor also*
> *gathered around Absalom and struck him and*
> *killed him.*
>   *Then Joab blew the trumpet, so the troops*
> *stopped chasing the Israelites. Then Joab's men*
> *took Absalom's body and threw it into a large*
> *pit in the forest and filled the pit with many*
> *stones. All the Israelites ran away to their*
> *homes. (2 Samuel 18:14-17, NCV)*

He killed the son of the king and got rid of the body. Joab was a merciless man of military.

We see the carnage. A raped daughter, a son murdered by another son, and now the death of that son. Wow.

As we close out this chapter, take into account your life. Or better yet, David's hidden life!

How much trouble for a one-night adulterous affair?

I am sure you believe that a little fling, an extra drink, a little skimming off the books, and all other lapses in morality will not lead to such consequences.

David is proof there are long lasting consequences for sin.

Let's see how David responded after he was victorious in his battle with his son. The result led to the death of his son.

The king was overcome with emotion. He went up to the room over the gateway and burst into tears. And as he went, he cried, "O my son Absalom! My son, my son Absalom! If only I had died instead of you! O Absalom, my son, my son." (2 Samuel 18:33, NLT)

He wept and almost lost his kingship as a result. You see Joab, the army, the supporters of David saw Absalom as a rebellious, dangerous threat. They believed the death of Absalom meant victory to David.

How did David view Absalom?

David saw him as his son.
The Sword will not depart from your household.
It was so unnecessary. It all could have been avoided.
Where are you in your life?

Chapter 16 Questions to Ponder

1. What convicted you about this chapter?

2. Do you believe that we truly reap what we sow?

3. How can you relate with the pain David suffered in this chapter?

4. Is there a way you can make decisions right now to avoid suffering great pain?

5. What is the main thing you will repent of after reading this chapter?

Answers to end of chapter questions

Chapter 17

David: A Man after the Heart of God

After the last few chapters it is time for some encouragement. David was the choice for king by the Lord because he was a man after the heart of God. We have looked at his failures and shortcomings. He was far from perfect. He, like us, made bad decisions and experienced failure.

We have had the opportunity to see the consequences of his sin. We have seen the failings he had had as a father. We have viewed the atrocious behavior and lives of his children. We have glossed through the ugly and warts of this man's life. It is meant to convict us and serve as a warning.

Please heed the warning!

Praise the Lord, the grace of Hashem helped in David's spiritual recovery. He brought a semblance of leadership back to the throne. He lived and saw the growth of his successor, his son Solomon.

The goal at the end of his life was to prepare and equip young Solomon with the materials to build the home for Jehovah, the temple, and to lead and shepherd the people of God.

Let's look at the end of David's reign and life.

> *David said, "The temple of the Lord God must be built right here at this threshing place. And the altar for offering sacrifices will also be here." (1 Chronicles 22:1, 5–19, CEV)*

David began to make all the preparations for his life's desire, the building of a home for the Most High. He was not the one to build it but he was going to do all he could to make sure it was an exemplary beautiful temple. He made elaborate plans. He did all he could to set up his son for victory.

> *He said, "The temple for the Lord must be great, so that everyone in the world will know about it. But since my son Solomon is young and has no experience, I will make sure that everything is ready for the temple to be built."*
> *That's why David did all these things before he died. (1 Chronicles 22:5, CEV)*

He was going to make sure he poured the last ounces of his life into his son to make up for the mistakes suffered with the other children. In a sense, the consequences he endured with his other sons lead him to devote time in young Solomon. The seed of his initial sin turned into his successor to the throne. That is the grace of God.

> *David sent for his son Solomon and told him to build a temple for the Lord God of Israel. He said:*

He confided his dreams, desires, and the Will of Hashem to his young, inexperienced son. He revealed the plans of God for his home.

> *My son, I wanted to build a temple where the Lord my God would be worshiped. But some time ago, he told me, "David, you have killed too many people and have fought too many battles. That's why you are not the one to build my temple. But when your son becomes king, I will give him peace throughout his kingdom. His name will be Solomon, because during his rule I will keep Israel safe and peaceful.*

Solomon will build my temple. He will be like a son to me, and I will be like a father to him. In fact, one of his descendants will always rule in Israel." (1 Chronicles 22:6-10, CEV)

How encouraging and inspiring to be told.

Solomon, my son, I now pray that the Lord your God will be with you and keep his promise to help you build a temple for him. May he give you wisdom and knowledge, so that you can rule Israel according to his Law. If you obey the laws and teachings that the Lord gave Moses, you will be successful. Be strong and brave and don't get discouraged or be afraid of anything. (1 Chronicles 22:11-13, CEV)

He instilled his faith and heart for the Lord in Solomon. He instructed him to know and allow the power of God to lead him. He implored Solomon to seek the true Father and crave for his wisdom to know the word and lead by the word of God. He pleaded with him to live in obedience to the word and not his own thoughts. He desired his son to avoid his mistakes and failures. He desired that his son be successful and brave. He warned him to be a man of faith and not fear. It was the ultimate handing down of advice from father to son. It was much more from one king to his successor. He encouraged him in the building of the temple.

I have all the supplies you'll need to build the temple: You have four thousand tons of gold and forty thousand tons of silver. There's also plenty of wood, stone, and more bronze and iron than I could weigh. Ask for anything else you need. (1 Chronicles 22:14, CEV)

He let his young son know that all has been provided and thought out for this great endeavor. He had all he needed. He would have all the help and support he would need.

> *I have also assigned men who will cut and lay the stone. And there are carpenters and people who are experts in working with gold, silver, bronze, and iron. You have plenty of workers to do the job. Now get started, and I pray that the Lord will be with you in your work. (1 Chronicles 22:15-16, CEV)*

He made the preparations for building the temple and the road to glorifying the Most High.

> *David then gave orders for the leaders of Israel to help Solomon. (1 Chronicles 22:17, CEV)*

He reminded the people of his own calling and the victories God had granted him. He implored all of the people to complete the task of building the temple and the challenge to honor and obey the Lord.

> *David said:*
> *The Lord our God has helped me defeat all the people who lived here before us, and he has given you peace from all your enemies. Now this land belongs to the Lord and his people. (1 Chronicles 22:18, CEV)*

David reflected on the blessings bestowed on him from the Lord. He declared the Lord was the one who delivered victory in battle and peace.

He encouraged his son to devote himself to God. He gave great council. He mentored and helped his son in order to prepare him for the kingdom. David did all Saul was unwilling to do.

He called him to the Lord.

Obey the Lord your God with your heart and soul. Begin work on the temple to honor him, so that the sacred chest and the things used for worship can be kept there. (1 Chronicles 22:19, CEV)

He is advising all of us on the key to a victorious life.

After David had lived long and was old, he made his son Solomon the new king of Israel. (1 Chronicles 23:1, NCV)

He crowned his son as the next king of Israel.

1 Chronicles 28:4–21 (NCV)

David spoke in front of the people of Israel.
He reminded the people of his calling and their calling as well.

"But the Lord, the God of Israel, chose me from my whole family to be king of Israel forever. He chose the tribe of Judah to lead, and from the people of Judah, he chose my father's family. From that family God was pleased to make me king of Israel. (1 Chronicles 28:4, NCV)

He was the choice of God to be king.
He declared that Hashem chose Solomon.

The Lord has given me many sons, and from those sons he has chosen Solomon to be the new king of Israel. Israel is the Lord's kingdom. The Lord said to me, 'Your son Solomon will build my Temple and its courtyards. I have chosen Solomon to be my son, and I will be his father. He is obeying my laws and commands now.

If he continues to obey them, I will make his kingdom strong forever.'" (1 Chronicles 28:5-7, NCV)

He declared to all the people.

David said, "Now, in front of all Israel, the assembly of the Lord, and in the hearing of God, I tell you these things: Be careful to obey all the commands of the Lord your God. Then you will keep this good land and pass it on to your descendants forever. (1 Chronicles 28:8, NCV)

We are all called to obey the commands of the Lord. No one is exempt.

"And you, my son Solomon, accept the God of your father. Serve him completely and willingly, because the Lord knows what is in everyone's mind. He understands everything you think. If you go to him for help, you will get an answer. But if you turn away from him, he will leave you forever. Solomon, you must understand this. The Lord has chosen you to build the Temple as his holy place. Be strong and finish the job." (1 Chronicles 28:9-10, NCV)

David gave Solomon his calling. He decreed to him to serve the Lord willingly. If he did, the Lord will be with him and provide him with all he needs as the king. He warns him of the consequences if he did not obey.

He then detailed the process of building the temple. It is amazing how detailed he was. He made all the preparations, and now ordered the fulfilling of the desire of his heart, which his son would perform.

Then David gave his son Solomon the plans for building the Temple and the courtyard around the Temple. They included its buildings, its storerooms, its upper rooms, its inside rooms, and the place where the people's sins were removed. David gave him plans for everything he had in mind: the courtyards around the Lord's Temple and all the rooms around it, the Temple treasuries, and the treasuries of the holy items used in the Temple. David gave Solomon directions for the groups of the priests and Levites. David told him about all the work of serving in the Temple of the Lord and about the items to be used in the Temple service that were made of gold or silver. David told Solomon how much gold or silver should be used to make each thing. David told him how much gold to use for each gold lampstand and its lamps and how much silver to use for each silver lampstand and its lamps. The different lampstands were to be used where needed. David told how much gold should be used for each table that held the holy bread and how much silver should be used for the silver tables. He told how much pure gold should be used to make the forks, bowls, and pitchers and how much gold should be used to make each gold dish. He told how much silver should be used to make each silver dish and how much pure gold should be used for the altar of incense. He also gave Solomon the plans for the chariot of the golden creatures that spread their wings over the Ark of the Agreement with the Lord. (1 Chronicles 28:11-18, NCV)

What a complete description. David dreamt of this day.

In an earlier chapter, we looked at David's reaction to having the Lord say "no" to his dream desire. Here we truly see why out of all the people the Lord chose David as his choice to be the king of his people.

> *David said, "All these plans were written with the Lord guiding me. He helped me understand everything in the plans." (1 Chronicles 28:19, NCV)*

As was the custom of the king he gave all the honor and glory to Jehovah.

> *David also said to his son Solomon, "Be strong and brave, and do the work. Don't be afraid or discouraged, because the Lord God, my God, is with you. He will not fail you or leave you until all the work for the Temple of the Lord is finished. (1 Chronicles 28:20, NCV)*

All children desire this type of instruction from their father's. David inspired faith and courage in his son. Let the Lord lead you.

> *The groups of the priests and Levites are ready for all the work on the Temple of God. Every skilled worker is ready to help you with all the work. The leaders and all the people will obey every command you give." (1 Chronicles 28:21, NCV)*

He reminded Solomon he will be supported as the king.

David Praises God for the Last Time

> *Then, in front of everyone, David sang praises to the Lord: (1 Chronicles 29:10–20, CEV)*

David, for the last time, praised the Most High. As you read, consider the life that David led.

Take a moment to contemplate his beginning, his victory over Goliath, his victory in battle, his kinship with Jonathan, his dealings with Saul, his failures, his suffering, his path to the kingship, his devotion to God, and now his handing the torch to Solomon.

Consider his words and the heart behind them. He gave the glory to his Lord. His dedication and devotion at the end was as it was in the beginning. He began all alone with the sheep, and now he was with the sheep of Israel. This was the way to go out with the Most High!

> *I praise you forever, Lord! You are the God our ancestor Jacob worshiped.*

He praised Jehovah.

> *Your power is great, and your glory is seen everywhere in heaven and on earth. You are king of the entire world, and you rule with strength and power. You make people rich and powerful and famous. (1 Chronicles 29:10-12, CEV)*

He extolled the power of our God. He continued giving him all the glory and honor.

This is what our praise of the Lord should be.

> *We thank you, our God, and praise you. (1 Chronicles 29:13, CEV)*

He brought the reality that all is God's. We are just here like a mist.

> *But why should we be happy that we have given you these gifts? They belong to you, and we have*

280

only given back what is already yours. We are only foreigners living here on earth for a while, just as our ancestors were. And we will soon be gone, like a shadow that suddenly disappears. (1 Chronicles 29:14-15, CEV)

He continued his praise and honoring of God.

Our Lord God, we have brought all these things for building a temple to honor you. They belong to you, and you gave them to us. But we are happy, because everyone has voluntarily given you these things. You know what is in everyone's heart, and you are pleased when people are honest. Always make us eager to give, and help us be faithful to you, just as our ancestors Abraham, Isaac, and Jacob faithfully worshiped you. (1 Chronicles 29:16-18, CEV)

What a prayer. He prayed for his son.

And give Solomon the desire to completely obey your laws and teachings, and the desire to build the temple for which I have provided these gifts. (1 Chronicles 29:19, CEV)

He prayed for the people.

David then said to the people, "Now it's your turn to praise the Lord, the God your ancestors worshiped!" So everyone praised the Lord, and they bowed down to honor him and David their king. (1 Chronicles 29:20, CEV)

They all worshipped and praised the God of all.

We can look at some other dealings of David at the twilight of his life, but I want us to end the book with inspiration and encouragement. It is my desire one day to write a continuation in the life of David. It was now time for the man after the heart of God to step aside and let his son take the throne and be the king.

> *Then, for a second time, they made David's son Solomon king; they anointed him[m] as the Lord's ruler, and Zadok as the priest. Solomon sat on the Lord's throne as king in place of his father David. He prospered, and all Israel obeyed him. All the leaders and the mighty men, and all of King David's sons as well, pledged their allegiance to King Solomon. The Lord highly exalted Solomon in the sight of all Israel and bestowed on him such royal majesty as had not been bestowed on any king over Israel before him. (1 Chronicles 29:22–28, HCSB)*

The time came for David to no longer be king. I am so impressed with the way he went out. We praised him for his beginning, in the middle we saw his failures, and the ugly side that all of us possess, and now at the end, we are impressed by how he ends his reign and goes to the grave.

He did all he could to repent for his failures as a father and set up Solomon for great success.

He became king with a divided faithless country. He built up the territory ten times what he inherited. He developed a unified Israel. He defeated all of his enemies. Now, there was a time of peace. The Ark of the Covenant was brought back to where it belonged. The temple was going to be built. David led the people to worship the Most High and left it all to his successor Solomon. He did all this with the Most High by his side.

The overriding reality in his life was God was in control. He would learn to rely on the strength of our heavenly Father.

What a life.

The sacred scriptures described his life.

David son of Jesse was king over all Israel. He had ruled over Israel forty years—seven years in Hebron and thirty-three years in Jerusalem. David died when he was old. He had lived a good, long life and had received many riches and honors. His son Solomon became king after him. (1 Chronicles 29:26-28, NCV)

We have looked into the life of a man of God. I hope it was as faith building for you, the reader, as it was for me in writing it. As we end our time together, let's make it our aim and life's desire to be known as people who have hearts after the heart of God. Let's strive to be men and women devoted to the Most High like King David. Let's choose to answer, "A Leader's Call."

"To Follow the Messiah" will be coming soon. Until we meet again.

About the Author

Michael P. Waterman was born in Brooklyn, NY. After earning a Bachelors degree in Business Administration from the University of Central Florida, he spent over a decade working as a financial advisor. But his true profession was to carry the Word of God. He has served in ministry for over 20 years. He has been happily married to his wife Sherly for over 13 years.

This will be the first of a five-part series.

CPSIA information can be obtained
at www.ICGtesting.com
Printed in the USA
LVHW11*1118231018
594510LV00007B/89/P

9 781642 996425